Lecture Notes in Computer Science 15935

The series Lecture Notes in Computer Science (LNCS), including its subseries Lecture Notes in Artificial Intelligence (LNAI) and Lecture Notes in Bioinformatics (LNBI), has established itself as a medium for the publication of new developments in computer science and information technology research, teaching, and education.

LNCS enjoys close cooperation with the computer science R & D community, the series counts many renowned academics among its volume editors and paper authors, and collaborates with prestigious societies. Its mission is to serve this international community by providing an invaluable service, mainly focused on the publication of conference and workshop proceedings and postproceedings. LNCS commenced publication in 1973.

Ryosuke Yamanishi · Andréia Formico ·
Yuta Sugiura · Kohei Matsumura
Editors

Entertainment Computing – ICEC 2025 IFIP TC 14 Workshops

Tokyo, Japan, August 27–30, 2025
Proceedings

 Springer

Editors
Ryosuke Yamanishi ⓘD
Kansai University
Osaka, Japan

Andréia Formico ⓘD
University of Fortaleza
Fortaleza, Brazil

Yuta Sugiura ⓘD
Keio University
Tokyo, Japan

Kohei Matsumura ⓘD
Ritsumeikan University
Osaka, Japan

ISSN 0302-9743   ISSN 1611-3349 (electronic)
Lecture Notes in Computer Science
ISBN 978-3-032-02533-3   ISBN 978-3-032-02534-0 (eBook)
https://doi.org/10.1007/978-3-032-02534-0

This Springer imprint is published by the registered company Springer Nature Switzerland AG
The registered company address is: Gewerbestrasse 11, 6330 Cham, Switzerland

Preface

This volume presents the proceedings of the workshops held at the 24th IFIP International Conference on Entertainment Computing (IFIP ICEC 2025), which took place in Tokyo, Japan, from August 27 to 30, 2025, hosted by Nihon University.

As a long-standing academic event in the fields of entertainment computing and interactive media, ICEC has continually fostered interdisciplinary dialogue through a diverse range of workshop programs. Recognizing the increasing importance and depth of these workshops, this year we decided to publish them in a separate proceedings volume.

At ICEC 2025, six workshops were proposed and underwent a peer review process led by juries headed by Workshop Chairs. Each workshop proposal received three reviews. All six workshops were accepted and held during the conference. Five workshop organizers chose to include their workshop descriptions in this proceedings volume, while one workshop opted not to publish their proposal.

These workshops provided focused and interactive venues for researchers, designers, and practitioners to explore new ideas, present ongoing work, and foster interdisciplinary collaboration.

Among the workshops, AERS 2025 (Accessibility and Empowerment Research Summit) included a call for papers. The submitted papers underwent a peer review process conducted by Program Committee members consisting of workshop organizers. Each paper received three reviews, and ten papers were initially accepted. However, due to author withdrawals, seven papers are included in this proceedings volume.

We extend our heartfelt appreciation to all the workshop organizers for their dedication, to the authors for their inspiring submissions, and to the reviewers for their thoughtful and timely feedback. We also thank the ICEC organizing committee and the local team at Nihon University for their generous support.

We hope this volume will serve as a valuable record of the innovative discussions and collaborations that took place at ICEC 2025 and contribute to the future development of the entertainment computing field.

July 2025

Ryosuke Yamanishi
Andréia Formico
Yuta Sugiura
Kohei Matsumura

Organization

Program Committee

Esteban Clua	Universidade Federal Fluminense, Brazil
Jerome Dupire	CNAM – CEDRIC, France
Andréia Formico	University of Fortaleza, Brazil
Jun Hu	Eindhoven University of Technology, The Netherlands
Jingya Li	Beijing Jiaotong University, China
Yuta Sugiura	Keio University, Japan
Thomas Westin	Stockholm University, Sweden
Mengru Xue	Zhejiang University, Ningbo, China
Cheng Yao	Zhejiang University, China
Tengjia Zuo	Hong Kong University of Science and Technology, China

Contents

Workshops

Integrating and Assessing Games for Health Deployments in Healthcare Settings via Implementation Science Frameworks

Elena Bertozzi[1]([✉]) [iD], Jannicke Baalsrud Hauge[2,3] [iD], Barbara Göbl[4] [iD],
and Clara Bertozzi-Villa[5]

[1] Quinnipiac University, Mt. Carmel Drive, Hamden, CT 06518, USA
elena.bertozzi@qu.edu

[2] BIBA – Bremer Institut für Produktion und Logistik GmbH, Hochschulring 20, 28359 Bremen, Germany
jmbh@kth.se

[3] Royal Institute of Technology, Kvarnbergagatan 12, Södertälje, Sweden

[4] Centre for Teacher Education, University of Vienna, 1090 Vienna, Austria
barbara.goebl@univie.ac.at

[5] Division of Maternal Fetal Medicine, Department of Obstetrics and Gynecology and Women's Health, Montefiore Einstein, Bronx, USA
cbertozz@montefiore.org

Abstract. Although many games for health (GFH) have been validated as effective means of improving patient outcomes, to date, there are few large-scale deployments of them in healthcare settings. Acceptance of GFH in healthcare settings requires rigorous outcomes collection and analysis that justify the cost and effort required to create and deploy them. Implementation science frameworks can be used as a means of enabling stakeholder acceptance of innovative digital interventions. This paper discusses the process of using implementation science frameworks to facilitate and assess deployments of games for health in healthcare settings. Based on past successful deployments, we suggest a framework for developing and deploying such games.

Keywords: games for health · serious games · outcomes assessment · implementation science

1 Introduction

Interactive digital media, specifically games, are validated tools for reaching and engaging audiences because they include art, narratives, voice-overs, sound effects, animations, simulated worlds, and other features that allow information to be communicated contextually and understood through practice [1, 2]. They can be delivered via devices (phones and tablets) that are familiar and easy to use. PubMed now lists hundreds of validated studies demonstrating the efficacy and utility of games and gamification for pro-health

R. Yamanishi et al. (Eds.): ICEC 2025 Workshops, LNCS 15935, pp. 3–6, 2025.
https://doi.org/10.1007/978-3-032-02534-0_1

behavior modification, knowledge gain, and increasing health literacy and self-efficacy [3, 4]. There are many obstacles to the large-scale implementation of games in healthcare which can be overcome through careful planning and coordination. The process requires buy-in from stakeholders including healthcare providers, educators, and policymakers. Implementation science research frameworks provide models for organizing research inclusive of assessment of intervention efficacy and adoption by practitioners [5–7]. Bertozzi et al. have established track records of using games for health to improve healthcare outcomes demonstrating how to effectively integrate digital technology into current standard of care practice in experimental settings [8, 9].

2 Discussion

Although patients are now routinely invited to download apps and provided with tablets in healthcare settings, the use of these is largely limited to managing appointments, prescriptions, and communicating with providers. Many health providers have installed technology such as computers and tablets in examination rooms, but these are used primarily by providers who interface with electronic record systems. Patients still spend hours sitting in waiting rooms prior to appointments and then in examination rooms waiting for providers to arrive surrounded by technology that is not being used to educate them about their care. They may also have unanswered questions about procedures that they are uncomfortable asking. Games provided prior to the examination/appointment can help reduce waiting times, improve awareness and understanding and facilitate communication with caregivers.

One of the obstacles to wide adoption of digital game-based learning (DGBL) is related to rigorous outcomes assessment, including the handling of sensitive data. Given that deployments are costly, it is vital that serious game developers have a clear understanding of how the desired behavior change can be measured and assessed. Although many studies of game-based learning have been published, few of these are clinical trials with rigorous outcomes assessment. Making the case for the utility and efficacy of such interventions to healthcare providers requires careful planning in terms of the scope of the intervention, pre/post assessments, and understanding the role of the staff and the environment in ensuring the successful adoption and use of the intervention. Our process is informed by the Exploration, Preparation, Implementation, Sustainment (EPIS) framework to ensure consideration of the complex interactions between game interventions, the intended audience, and healthcare providers [10]. Within this framework Moulin, et.al. Found that: "...concepts that should be considered include those relating to the process of implementation (the stages and steps), the innovation to be implemented, the context in which the implementation is to occur (divided into various numbers of domains), influencing factors, strategies, and evaluations." [11].

Based on our past experience with such deployments, we recommend the following areas of emphasis in the planning and deployment of GFH in healthcare settings:

2.1 Stakeholder Buy-in

At the earliest possible stage in the game development process, any healthcare professional that will be affected by the proposed deployment should be included in the design process. If a game is to be made available to patients in waiting rooms, for example, the secretaries in the office, nurses who meet and guide patients, and physicians and other providers who will interface with patients should all be included in pre-implementation focus groups. There should be clarity from all stakeholders about the goals of the deployment, desired patient outcomes, and assessment procedures. Staff will have important contributions to make about the best way to deliver the GFH to the target audience. Patients in the target audience should also be interviewed and included in focus groups and iterative testing. Over the course of testing, it is crucial to determine how deployment can save time and make all stakeholders' processes more efficient. If it becomes clear that this will not be the case, it may be better to revisit the proposal. A deployment cannot succeed if it disrupts the already complex processes in healthcare deployment.

2.2 Hardware/Software Considerations

Once a process for delivering the GFH to the target audience has been proposed, the design team should carefully consider the hardware and software deployment strategy. In a low-cost, low-resource environment, for example, it may be best to provide the intervention on Android tablets or computers in a shared space but in an area where they can have some privacy. Android and PC operating systems allow for the easy sharing and installation of software. In other settings, using Apple IOS delivery systems may be appropriate. In the latter case, there should be a clear understanding of the processing and requirements of distributing materials through the Apple App store (the review process is lengthy and certain kinds of content are not permitted). Practical considerations including stands to hold tablets and protect them from theft, headphones for audio, and a plan for who to call to resolve technical glitches should be included in the planning.

2.3 Outcomes Assessment Strategies

One of the most compelling reasons to use GFH is that knowledge assessments and other kinds of anonymized data collection can be embedded in the gameplay [4][12]. Rather than using pre/post questionnaires or other traditional means of collecting data about patient knowledge, games can be designed to challenge players as they play. A "tutorial" that teaches players how to play the game can also assess baseline knowledge. As players play the game, other in-game metrics can be stored which track how much time players spent engaging with different parts of the game, whether they re-played different sections, and if they requested or used help. Carefully designed games can collect very useful anonymized data about the topic of interest.

3 Conclusion

Games for health hold significant promise for improving the quality of patient education, facilitating conversations between patients and providers, and promoting pro-health behavior choices. The process of successfully deploying these interventions in healthcare settings is complicated and should be informed by numerous factors.

References

1. Squire, K.D.: Video games in education. Games Simul. **2**(1), 49–62 (2003)
2. Steinkuehler, C., Squire, K., Barab, S.A.: Games, learning, and society : learning and meaning in the digital age. In: Learning in Doing. Cambridge University Press, Cambridge (2012)
3. Damaševičius, R., Maskeliūnas, R., Blažauskas, T.: Serious games and gamification in healthcare: a meta-review. Information **14**(2), 105 (2023). https://doi.org/10.3390/info14 020105
4. Nylén-Eriksen, M., et al.: Game-thinking; utilizing serious games and gamification in nursing education – a systematic review and metaanalysis. BMC Med. Educ. **25**(1), 140 (2025). https://doi.org/10.1186/s12909-024-06531-7
5. McGuier, E.A., et al.: Teamwork and implementation of innovations in healthcare and human service settings: a systematic review. Implement. Sci. **19**(1), 49 (2024). https://doi.org/10.1186/s13012-024-01381-9
6. Damschroder, L.J., Reardon, C.M., Widerquist, M.A.O., Lowery, J.: The updated consolidated framework for implementation research based on user feedback. Implement. Sci. **17**(1), 75 (2022). https://doi.org/10.1186/s13012-022-01245-0
7. Proctor, E., et al.: Outcomes for implementation research: conceptual distinctions, measurement challenges, and research agenda. Adm. Policy Ment. Health **38**(2), 65–76 (2011). https://doi.org/10.1007/s10488010-0319-7
8. Bertozzi, E., Bertozzi-Villa, A., Padankatti, S., Sridhar, A.: Outcomes assessment pitfalls: challenges to quantifying knowledge gain in a sex education game. Gates Open Res. **4**, 73 (2021). https://doi.org/10.12688/gatesopenres.13129.3
9. Bertozzi, E., et al.: Supporting contraceptive self-care and reproductive empowerment with a digital health game in Barbados: development and pre-implementation study for what's my method? Gates Open Res. **8**, 47 (2024). https://doi.org/10.12688/gatesopenres.15376.2
10. Nilsen, P., Birken, S.A. (eds.) Handbook on Implementation Science. Edward Elgar Publishing, Cheltenham (2020). https://doi.org/10.4337/9781788975995
11. Moullin, J.C., Sabater-Hernández, D., Fernandez-Llimos, F., Benrimoj, S.I.: A systematic review of implementation frameworks of innovations in healthcare and resulting generic implementation framework. Health Res. Policy Syst. **13**(1), 16 (2015). https://doi.org/10.1186/s12961-015-0005-z
12. Maddison, R., et al.: Feasibility of using games to improve healthy lifestyle knowledge in youth aged 9–16 years at risk for type 2 diabetes: pilot randomized controlled trial. JMIR Form Res **6**(6), e33089 (2022). https://doi.org/10.2196/33089

Design Expertise in Entertainment Computing Practices

Nandhini Giri[1]([⊠]) [iD] and Erik Stolterman[2] [iD]

[1] Purdue University, West Lafayette, IN 47907, USA
girin@purdue.edu
[2] Indiana University, Bloomington, IN 47405, USA

Abstract. This half-day workshop will introduce participants to the theoretical foundations of design expertise and maturity frameworks to develop enjoyable and sustainable design processes in interactive entertainment practices. Participants will learn about the stages of design expertise, identify issues with existing design processes and develop a strategy to improve their own processes.

Keywords: Design Expertise · Design Maturity Frameworks · Design Processes

1 Introduction

1.1 Workshop Summary, Short Review of State of the Art, Motivation, and Goals

In recent years, an increasing number of organizations are adopting a design mindset to navigate through technological, economical, and market shifts. One of the major organizational initiatives that is part of this design transformation is the adoption of design expertise and maturity models, to make organizations more design-focused and user friendly. Maturity frameworks provide a structure for assessing key performance metrics of an organization and provide guidelines for assessment and growth in various areas of an organization. Design maturity frameworks suggest ways to adopt a designerly mindset in the various operations of the organization including processes, practices, products, and people.

The interactive entertainment industry comprising games, interactive media, animated content and mixed reality application development, incorporates several aspects of design practices in the development process - both in the context of educational and professional settings. Entertainment computing practices bring together design approaches and traditions from several fields. This necessitates a discussion of design expertise development specific to the field of entertainment computing. How to incorporate a designerly mindset in my existing work? How to identify motivating factors for a sustainable design process? How to develop metrics to assess my progress as an individual and a team?

This half-day workshop is designed with a goal of initiating these discussions in the field of entertainment computing. The workshop introduces participants to human

R. Yamanishi et al. (Eds.): ICEC 2025 Workshops, LNCS 15935, pp. 7–10, 2025.
https://doi.org/10.1007/978-3-032-02534-0_2

factors that promote or inhibit the enjoyability of design processes. Discipline-specific design practices will be discussed, followed by group activities to co-design metrics to assess and improve the adoption of design thinking and expertise development. Participants will bring a position paper, a case study of a recent design project or a pictorial description of their design process. Prework for this workshop is optional, and participants joining the workshop without this pre-work experience will be provided with the necessary material to work on during the workshop. Individual presentations will generate discussions, critiques and reflections. The goal of this workshop is for participants to identify their own motivational approaches to entertainment computing practices and co-design maturity models to assess their process. The workshop authors will facilitate the session and are trained in leading discussions, hands-on activities, and expertise discussing topics related to design expertise and entertainment practices. The workshop activities will extend further into scholarly publications and expertise development guidelines for practitioners.

1.2 Workshop Format (an Activity Plan and Its Rationale Towards the Goals).

The session is structured to include topic presentation, individual and group activities, and follow-up discussions. Workshop structure follows a 50 min activity + 10 min break format for 3 hours.

Hour #1

- Topic presentation introducing concepts of enjoyable and non-enjoyable factors in design practices. (20 min)
- Individual activity to identify enjoyable and non-enjoyable factors in design practices. (30 min)
- Break (10 min)

Hour #2

- Whiteboard activity grouping enjoyable and non-enjoyable factors, followed by a discussion of discipline specific design practices in entertainment computing (50 min)
- Break (10 min)

Hour #3

- Topic presentation introducing concepts of design maturity and expertise development in professional design practices. (20 min)
- Individual activity to identify areas of design expertise development in personal practices and processes. [Alternatively: Participants will give a brief presentation of their workshop submission] (30 min)
- Break (10 min)

Additional Activities

- Group activity to co-design assessment metrics in discipline-specific design practices. (25 min)
- Group discussion on an agenda for developing design expertise in entertainment computing practices and next steps. (25 min)

- Wrap up (10 min)

1.3 Workshop Format for Participant Enrollment (e.g. Position Papers, Prior Expression of Interest, or Other Applicable Requirements for Planning and Organization)

A website will be created for participants to read through articles related to design expertise, maturity models, and designing user-friendly processes. Participants have the option of providing prior expressions of interest by contacting the workshop authors through email. This gives participants the opportunity to reflect over their own design processes and roles played in entertainment computing practices. Participants will be asked to submit a written position paper, case study of a recent project or pictorial of their design process prior to the workshop. Alternatively, participants can also join the workshop without the pre-work/preparation for the workshop. These participants will be provided with preliminary material to work on during the workshop.

1.4 Profile of Participants (and Estimated Number of Participants)

The workshop aims to identify human factors that motivate individuals and organizations in developing design processes that generate enjoyable and sustainable workplace experiences. The content of the session will benefit novice to experienced educators, professionals, and students to rethink their own professional practices in terms of design expertise development and motivational processes in classrooms and professional settings. Typical profiles of participants will vary from students reflecting over their own design practices, educators incorporating intentional structures in classroom design practices, and seasoned entertainment professionals making team-level decisions for their designers.

An estimated number of participants vary between 15–25 participants.

1.5 Expected Workshop Outcomes (Proceedings, Special Issue of Journals, Project Proposals, etc.)

The workshop organizers will produce a concluding document from the workshop session. Discussion summaries and images of whiteboard activities from the individual/group activities will be interpreted and analyzed for writing the concluding document. Workshop organizers plan to create an online community through the workshop website (and Discord) to continue conversations after the workshop. Participants will be encouraged to further develop their ideas and plan to publish the findings in (a) an academic journal and (b) report format for educators, researchers and professional designers.

1.6 Any Special Technical or Logistical Requirements for the Workshop

Whiteboards with markers, post it notes, computer/laptop, and projector to present the slide-deck are needed to facilitate the workshop session.

References

1. Enkel, E., Bell, J., Hogenkamp, H.: Open innovation maturity framework. Int. J. Innov. Manag. **15**(06), 1161–1189 (2011)
2. Giri, N.:. An Enjoyable Approach to Design Expertise in Gaming and Interactive Entertainment Industry Practices (Doctoral dissertation, Indiana University) (2021)
3. Giri, N., Stolterman, E.: Systems approach to designing an enjoyable process for game designers. In: HCI International 2020–Late Breaking Papers: Cognition, Learning and Games: 22nd HCI International Conference, HCII 2020, Copenhagen, Denmark, 19–24 July 2020, Proceedings 22, pp. 669–687. Springer, Heidelberg (2020)
4. Giri, N., Stolterman, E.: An analysis of design maturity models used in design organizations. In: Lockton, D., Lenzi, S., Hekkert, P., Oak, A., Sádaba, J., Lloyd, P. (eds.), DRS2022, Bilbao, Spain, 25 June–3 July 2022 (2022). https://doi.org/10.21606/drs.2022.276
5. Invision. The New Design Frontier (2018). https://www.invisionapp.com/designbetter/design-maturity-model/
6. Jörg, B.: Maturity models for IT management-a procedure model and its application/Jörg Becker, Ralf Knackstedt, Jens Pöppelbuß. Bus. Inf. Syst. Eng. **1**(3), 213–222 (2009)
7. Merholz, P., Skinner, K.: Org design for design orgs: Building and managing in-house design teams. O'Reilly Media, Inc., Santa Rosa (2016)
8. Pöppelbuß, J., Röglinger, M.: What makes a useful maturity model? A framework of general design principles for maturity models and its demonstration in business process management (2011)
9. Vallerand, J., Lapalme, J., Moïse, A.: Analysing enterprise architecture maturity models: a learning perspective. Enterp. Inf. Syst. **11**(6), 859–883 (2017)

Exploring Gender Bias in LLM-Generated Hero and Heroine Narratives

Irene C. E. van Blerck[1,2]($\boxtimes$) (ID) and Edirlei Soares de Lima[1] (ID)

[1] Academy for AI, Games and Media, Breda University of Applied Sciences, Breda, The Netherlands
blerck.i@buas.nl, soaresdelima.e@buas.nl

[2] Department of Computer Science, University of Antwerp, Antwerp, Belgium

Abstract. Narrative structures such as the Hero's Journey and Heroine's Journey have long influenced how characters, themes, and roles are portrayed in storytelling. When used to guide narrative generation in systems powered by Large Language Models (LLMs), these structures may interact with model-internal biases, reinforcing traditional gender norms. This workshop examines how protagonist gender and narrative structure shape storytelling outcomes in LLM-based storytelling systems. Through hands-on experiments and guided analysis, participants will explore gender representation in LLM-generated stories, perform counterfactual modifications, and evaluate how narrative interpretations shift when character gender is altered. The workshop aims to foster interdisciplinary collaborations, inspire novel methodologies, and advance research on fair and inclusive AI-driven storytelling in games and interactive media.

Keywords: Storytelling · Large Language Models · Gender Bias · Counterfactuals

1 Introduction

The increasing adoption of Large Language Models (LLMs) in storytelling raises important concerns about the persistence and reinforcement of gender biases. Recent studies have demonstrated that LLMs frequently reflect and, in some cases, amplify gender stereotypes present in the training data [6]. In narrative generation, prior research has shown that LLMs tend to associate female characters with themes of family and appearance while portraying them with significantly less agency than male characters [16]. Furthermore, the influence of literary genres and narrative conventions on LLM-generated texts complicates efforts to disentangle biases inherent to Artificial Intelligence (AI) models from those embedded in the storytelling traditions they replicate [5]. While some studies suggest that LLMs may introduce progressive gender representations in certain contexts [1], others reveal persistent biases in how AI systems associate gender with professions and social interactions [17]. Beyond gender, research has

© IFIP International Federation for Information Processing 2025
Published by Springer Nature Switzerland AG 2025
R. Yamanishi et al. (Eds.): ICEC 2025 Workshops, LNCS 15935, pp. 11–16, 2025.
https://doi.org/10.1007/978-3-032-02534-0_3

also identified structural biases in narrative outcomes, such as a strong preference for positive endings in game-related stories [21, 22].

Despite these findings, existing work has largely overlooked the role of narrative structures in shaping gender biases in AI-generated storytelling. Most studies focus on word-level associations, thematic biases, or profession-based stereotypes but do not systematically examine how protagonist gender interacts with structured storytelling frameworks, such as the Hero's Journey [2] and Heroine's Journey [18]. Prior work has demonstrated the importance of narrative structures in managing character arcs and plot progression, particularly in interactive environments [9–11], yet little attention has been given to how these structures may influence gender stereotypes when operationalized in LLM-based generation systems. Furthermore, prior research has not applied counterfactual estimation to assess causal effects, leaving open the question of whether LLM biases primarily stem from this interaction or if they are significantly influenced by other, potentially unobserved factors.

Building on our experience developing LLM-based narrative generation systems [7, 8, 12–15], this workshop aims to address key gaps in current research by providing a hands-on exploration of gender bias in LLM-generated storytelling. It focuses specifically on the interaction between protagonist gender and narrative structure – an area that remains underexamined despite its influence on the generated narratives. Participants will engage in practical experiments, including direct bias analysis and counterfactual generation using state-of-the-art LLMs. Additionally, the workshop will foster discussion on bias mitigation strategies, encouraging participants to discuss different approaches for addressing gender bias in AI-generated storytelling.

The workshop's key objectives are to:

1. Examine gender bias in LLM-generated narratives by analyzing protagonist representation in different narrative structures.
2. Evaluate the impact of counterfactual narrative generation as a methodology for identifying and quantifying gender bias in storytelling systems.
3. Explore different bias mitigation strategies, providing participants the opportunity to discuss and assess approaches for promoting fairer and more inclusive LLM-based storytelling systems.

By integrating insights from ethics, computational creativity, and interactive storytelling, this workshop aims to advance the discourse on responsible AI in narrative generation and contribute to shaping future storytelling technologies that transcend traditional gender biases.

2   Exploring Gender Bias in LLM-Generated Narratives

This section presents the practical and analytical activities through which gender bias in LLM-generated narratives is investigated. Building on recent advances in interactive storytelling and LLM-based narrative generation, we outline a structured exploration that combines hands-on experimentation, comparative analysis, and group discussion. The aim is to foster a deeper understanding of how narrative structures, protagonist gender, and model behavior interact to shape storytelling outputs.

2.1   Phase 1: Narrative Generation and Gender Bias Analysis

The exploration begins with the generation of fictional stories using Pattern-Teller [12,15], an AI-powered storytelling system guided by predefined narrative structures. Participants use the system to generate narratives based on neutral prompts and well-established narrative structures: the Hero's Journey [2] and the Heroine's Journey [18]. These generated narratives serve as the primary data for analysis.

Participants then evaluate the gender representation in their generated stories, focusing on protagonist identity, thematic associations, and role positioning. To complement qualitative interpretation, we apply the GenBit Score [20] – a metric for quantifying gender associations in text – using an interactive tool developed for this purpose. Through this process, participants identify patterns in how LLMs assign gender roles within given narratives and how these roles relate to societal stereotypes or literary conventions.

2.2   Phase 2: Counterfactual Narrative Generation and Structural Classification

In the second phase, we examine whether protagonist gender influences how LLMs interpret and classify stories in relation to the same narrative structures that guided their generation. To this end, participants apply a counterfactual approach using an LLM-assisted workflow, which modifies the gender of all characters in the stories they generated in Phase 1 while preserving all other narrative elements. These counterfactual versions serve as comparative counterparts to the factual narratives and form the basis for analyzing how shifts in gender representation may affect narrative classification outcomes.

Both the original and counterfactual narratives are then classified through an LLM-assisted workflow, using the same model that generated the stories. The classification prompt asks the model to determine whether each narrative aligns more closely with the Hero's Journey or the Heroine's Journey by comparing the story to key structural stages. Participants review the resulting classifications and analyze cases where a shift in protagonist gender leads to a different structural interpretation. This process offers insight into how gendered assumptions may influence model behavior, with a particular focus on recurring misclassification patterns and instances where stereotypical associations appear to override the narrative's actual content.

2.3   Phase 3: Bias Mitigation Strategies and Collective Reflection

The final phase involves a reflective group discussion on observed biases and potential strategies to mitigate them in LLM-driven storytelling systems. Drawing from examples generated during earlier phases, participants discuss diverse mitigation approaches. These include fine-tuning or Reinforcement Learning with Human Feedback (RLHF) [23], where models are aligned with human preferences through curated reward signals to discourage biased outputs; debiasing post-processing [3], which adjusts generated content to reduce stereotype exposure or gender imbalance; output filtering or re-ranking [19], where multiple generations are evaluated and filtered to select those that demonstrate more inclusive or balanced representations; and system-level interventions [4], which integrate external control layers or workflows that monitor and guide LLM behavior without altering the model itself. Ethical considerations – such as the trade-offs between creative freedom, fairness, and interpretability – are also critically discussed. This dialogue aims to seed future collaborations and encourage the development of new methodologies for fair and inclusive AI storytelling.

3   Expected Outcomes

This workshop aims to stimulate critical discussions on gender bias in LLM-generated narratives while equipping participants with practical skills to analyze and mitigate such biases. By engaging with hands-on experiments and structured discussions, attendees will gain insights into how narrative structures and protagonist gender influence the outputs of LLM-based storytelling systems. A key outcome is to raise awareness of the challenges in ensuring fair and unbiased LLM-generated narratives, particularly in entertainment applications such as games and interactive storytelling.

Beyond the immediate learning experience, this workshop is intended to facilitate new research collaborations and interdisciplinary projects. Insights gained from discussions may contribute to the development of new research initiatives, including collaborative publications and project proposals exploring strategies for mitigating bias in AI storytelling. We aim to facilitate networking opportunities that could lead to long-term collaborations between researchers, developers, and practitioners working in AI-driven creative fields.

As a tangible post-workshop outcome, we will invite interested participants to co-author a position or research paper summarizing workshop discussions, emergent insights, and open challenges. We also plan to form a working group to explore the possibility of forming a working group to develop project proposals focusing on bias mitigation in AI storytelling, with potential applications in game development, interactive narratives, and ethical AI research.

4   Conclusion

As LLM-based storytelling systems are increasingly used for narrative generation, examining how LLMs internalize and reproduce gender norms becomes a critical area of research. This workshop responds to that need by offering a collaborative environment where participants engage directly with LLM-generated narratives, observe how bias emerges in relation to narrative structure, and reflect on the broader implications for storytelling systems.

Rather than providing definitive solutions, this workshop emphasizes the open questions around fairness, creativity, and accountability in LLM-driven storytelling. By encouraging critical discussion and hands-on experimentation, it aims to lay the groundwork for sustained interdisciplinary research at the intersection of narrative theory, machine learning, and ethics. The insights developed through this workshop are intended not only to inform technical design but also to challenge and refine our collective understanding of what inclusive and responsible storytelling should look like in the age of generative AI.

Disclosure of Interests. The authors have no competing interests to declare that are relevant to the content of this workshop.

References

1. Begus, N.: Experimental narratives: a comparison of human crowdsourced storytelling and AI storytelling (2023). https://arxiv.org/abs/2310.12902
2. Campbell, J.: The Hero With a Thousand Faces. New World Library (2008)
3. Ghanbarzadeh, S., Huang, Y., Palangi, H., Moreno, R.C., Khanpour, H.: Gender-tuning: empowering fine-tuning for debiasing pre-trained language models. In: Rogers, A., Boyd-Graber, J., Okazaki, N. (eds.) Findings of the Association for Computational Linguistics: ACL 2023, Toronto, Canada, pp. 5448–5458. Association for Computational Linguistics (2023). https://doi.org/10.18653/v1/2023.findings-acl.336
4. Huang, D., Zhang, J.M., Bu, Q., Xie, X., Chen, J., Cui, H.: Bias testing and mitigation in LLM-based code generation. ACM Trans. Softw. Eng. Methodol. (2025). https://doi.org/10.1145/3724117
5. Jackson, D., Courneya, M.: Unreliable narrator: reparative approaches to harmful biases in AI storytelling for the he classroom and future creative industries. Braz. Creat. Ind. J. **3**(2), 59–75 (2023). https://doi.org/10.25112/bcij.v3i2.3540
6. Kotek, H., Dockum, R., Sun, D.: Gender bias and stereotypes in large language models. In: Proceedings of The ACM Collective Intelligence Conference, CI 2023, pp. 12–24. Association for Computing Machinery, New York (2023). https://doi.org/10.1145/3582269.3615599
7. de Lima, E.S., Casanova, M.A., Feijó, B., Furtado, A.L.: Semiotic structuring in movie narrative generation. In: Ciancarini, P., Di Iorio, A., Hlavacs, H., Poggi, F. (eds.) Entertainment Computing – ICEC 2023, pp. 161–175. Springer, Singapore (2023). https://doi.org/10.1007/978-981-99-8248-6_13
8. de Lima, E.S., Feijó, B., Casanova, M.A., Furtado, A.L.: ChatGeppetto - an AI-powered storyteller. In: Proceedings of the 22nd Brazilian Symposium on Games and Digital Entertainment, pp. 28–37. ACM (2024). https://doi.org/10.1145/3631085.3631302
9. de Lima, E.S., Feijó, B., Furtado, A.L.: Adaptive branching quests based on automated planning and story arcs. In: 2021 20th Brazilian Symposium on Computer Games and Digital Entertainment (SBGames), pp. 9–18 (2021). https://doi.org/10.1109/SBGames54170.2021.00012
10. de Lima, E.S., Feijó, B., Furtado, A.L.: Procedural generation of branching quests for games. Entertain. Comput. **43**, 100491 (2022). https://doi.org/10.1016/j.entcom.2022.100491

11. de Lima, E.S., Feijó, B., Furtado, A.L.: Managing the plot structure of character-based interactive narratives in games. Entertain. Comput. **47**, 100590 (2023). https://doi.org/10.1016/j.entcom.2023.100590

12. de Lima, E.S., Neggers, M.M.E., Casanova, M.A., Feijó, B., Furtado, A.L.: A pattern-oriented AI-powered approach to story composition. In: Figueroa, P., Di Iorio, A., Guzman del Rio, D., Gonzalez Clua, E.W., Cuevas Rodriguez, L. (eds.) Entertainment Computing – ICEC 2024, pp. 1–16. Springer, Cham (2024). https://doi.org/10.1007/978-3-031-74353-5_10

13. de Lima, E.S., Neggers, M.M.E., Furtado, A.L.: Multigenre AI-powered story composition (2025). https://arxiv.org/abs/2405.06685

14. de Lima, E.S., Neggers, M.M., Casanova, M.A., Furtado, A.L.: From images to stories: exploring player-driven narratives in games. In: Marto, A., Prada, R., Gouveia, P., Contreras-Espinosa, R., Gonçalves, A., Abrantes, E., Ribeiro, R. (eds.) Videogame Sciences and Arts, pp. 228–242. Springer, Cham (2025). https://doi.org/10.1007/978-3-031-81713-7_16

15. de Lima, E.S., Neggers, M.M., Feijó, B., Casanova, M.A., Furtado, A.L.: An AI-powered approach to the semiotic reconstruction of narratives. Entertain. Comput. **52**, 100810 (2025). https://doi.org/10.1016/j.entcom.2024.100810

16. Lucy, L., Bamman, D.: Gender and representation bias in GPT-3 generated stories. In: Proceedings of the Third Workshop on Narrative Understanding, pp. 48–55. Association for Computational Linguistics, Virtual (2021). https://doi.org/10.18653/v1/2021.nuse-1.5

17. Marin, A., Eger, M.: Towards evaluating profession-based gender bias in chatGPT and its impact on narrative generation. In: Farrokhimaleki, M., Rahmati, P., Saadat, K., Zhao, R. (eds.) Proceedings of the AIIDE Workshop on Intelligent Narrative Technologies co-located with the 20th AAAI Conference on Artificial Intelligence and Interactive Digital Entertainment (AIIDE 2024), Lexington, Kentucky, USA (2024)

18. Murdock, M.: The Heroine's Journey: Woman's Quest for Wholeness. Shambhala (1990)

19. Nouriinanloo, B., Lamothe, M.: Re-ranking step by step: investigating pre-filtering for re-ranking with large language models (2024). https://arxiv.org/abs/2406.18740

20. Sengupta, K., Maher, R., Groves, D., Olieman, C.: GenBiT: measure and mitigate gender bias in language datasets. Microsoft J. Appl. Pharm. Res. **16**, 63–71 (2021)

21. Taveekitworachai, P., et al.: What is waiting for us at the end? inherent biases of game story endings in large language models. In: Holloway-Attaway, L., Murray, J.T. (eds.) Interactive Storytelling, pp. 274–284. Springer, Cham (2023)

22. Taveekitworachai, P., Plupattanakit, K., Thawonmas, R.: Assessing inherent biases following prompt compression of large language models for game story generation. In: 2024 IEEE Conference on Games (CoG), pp. 1–4 (2024). https://doi.org/10.1109/CoG60054.2024.10645609

23. Ziegler, D.M., et al.: Fine-tuning language models from human preferences (2020). https://arxiv.org/abs/1909.08593

Accessibility and Empowerment Research Summit

Thomas Westin[1]([✉]) [iD], Jérôme Dupire[2] [iD], Esteban Clua[3] [iD], Mengru Xue[4] [iD],
Tengjia Zuo[5] [iD], Jingya Li[6] [iD], Cheng Yao[4] [iD], and Jun Hu[7] [iD]

[1] Dep. of Computer and Systems Sciences, Stockholm University, Kista, Sweden
`thomasw@dsv.su.se`
[2] CNAM, 292 Rue Saint-Martin, Paris, France
[3] Universidade Federal Fluminense, Rua Miguel de Frias, 9 Icaraí, Niteroi, RJ, Brazil
[4] Ningbo Global Innovation Center, Zhejiang University, No.1 South Qianhu Rd, Ningbo, China
[5] The Hong Kong University of Science and Technology (Guangzhou), No. 1 Du Xue Rd,
Guangzhou, China
[6] Beijing Jiaotong University, Shangyuancun No. 3, Beijing, China
[7] Eindhoven University of Technology, 5612 AZ Eindhoven, The Netherlands

Abstract. Following the successful workshops organized at ICEC 2024, this version aims to gather researchers in the fields of game accessibility and generative AI to explore gaps, opportunities, and challenges in advancing accessibility, inclusion, and empowerment through AI.

Keywords: Game Accessibility · Inclusive Design Processes · Accessible Controllers · Development Kits · Education · Therapeutic Tools · Participatory Design Platforms · Generative AI for Creating Social Value · Ethical Risks and Strategies · AI-driven Community Projects

1 Introduction

1.1 Background

This paper presents a joint effort of organizing a workshop addressing both accessibility and empowerment within entertainment computing, with a dual focus: 1) Game Accessibility, and 2) Empowerment through generative AI. While these are two distinct research areas that require a focused discussion, there are also overlaps where fruitful exchange of ideas and collaborations can emerge.

Game accessibility has evolved significantly during the last decade, both in research and in the industry. Progress includes accessible controllers, development kits, educational material, inclusive design processes and research about specific, often neglected groups such as deafblind gamers and people with cognitive disabilities. The Game Accessibility Conference[1] gathers developers and researchers in presentations and discussions.

---

[1] https://www.gaconf.com/.

© IFIP International Federation for Information Processing 2025
Published by Springer Nature Switzerland AG 2025
R. Yamanishi et al. (Eds.): ICEC 2025 Workshops, LNCS 15935, pp. 17–23, 2025.
https://doi.org/10.1007/978-3-032-02534-0_4

Research conferences also enable ad hoc meetings and of course, individual researchers collaborate on specific topics in various research efforts. However, there is a lack of an organized, continuously sustained effort to meet all or most peer researchers within this specific field of research, where this annual workshop intends to fill this gap in a long-term effort to advance the field and work together towards universal access in computer games as well as inclusive design processes.

Research about empowerment through generative AI recognizes that AI enhances efficiency, fosters collaboration, and optimizes resource allocation in underserved regions. However, it also raises conflicts such as intellectual property issues, debates over AI-generated content, and ethical concerns related to privacy, bias, and job displacement. While generative AI presents transformative potential in creating social value, its integration into accessibility and empowerment contexts remains underexplored. For instance, AI-driven tools are increasingly being used to develop accessible controllers, therapeutic applications, and educational resources, yet their ethical implications and long-term impacts on marginalized communities are not yet fully understood. The rapid advancement of generative AI technologies has outpaced regulatory frameworks, leading to unresolved tensions between innovation and responsibility.

1.2 Purpose and Goal

The purpose is to have peer researchers work together to identify gaps, opportunities, and challenges in game accessibility, inclusion, and empowerment through generative AI.

Thus, the workshop is open to all researchers and PhD students in the fields of games accessibility and empowerment, in a hybrid format to enable as many as possible to participate. The workshop also includes a call for contributions on dedicated papers in the field and publish peer reviewed and accepted papers as a separate chapter in the LNCS dedicated to ICEC 2025.

The goals of the workshop are: 1) Discuss submitted and accepted contributions from researchers and PhD students; 2) Outline research gaps, opportunities, and challenges, including possible collaborations; 3) Decide on a continuous academic forum format for advancing game accessibility and empowerment research.

2   Workshop Design

As point of departure, the call for papers forms the basis for the workshop but we also keep the workshop open for all attendees to have a fruitful discussion that extends beyond those who are already established in the field, such as students on different levels attending the conference. Here a brief introduction to game accessibility and empowerment through generative AI is presented, followed by the workshop layout.

2.1   A Brief Overview of Game Accessibility in Research

The Diverse Field of Game Accessibility

An overarching direction for game accessibility is the social model of disability [1], where accessibility is about removing unnecessary barriers for playing a game. However, game accessibility can be categorised in several different ways. For instance: 1) different groups of disabilities, such as visual, hearing, motor, cognitive and speech, similar to how the Game Accessibility Guidelines[2] are organized; 2) by input (joysticks, buttons, switches, voice commands, motion, location, and gaze control) or output modalities e.g. visuals (game world and objects, as well as user interface), auditory (e.g. music, sound effects, ambience, spatial) and haptic feedback (e.g. force, vibration); 3) by software and hardware solutions, where for instance various hardware controllers also need software for controller remapping, or gaze control that make use of software designed to work well with eye trackers, e.g. Eyemine by SpecialEffect[3]. Another example of this is MotionInput Games[4] where a web camera is repurposed as a motion-based input, i.e. touchless computing; 4) by generic (e.g. screen-reader) versus dedicated (e.g. recorded voice actors) approaches; 5) by different platforms such as games for PC, mobile, console, extended reality devices and more.

This list of categories is non-exhaustive and serves here only to raise some awareness of the variety and complexity of what game accessibility research need to consider. Furthermore, it can be argued that games often exceed the game itself, moving into creativity and work. Examples of this are sandbox games which basically are game editors, or e-sports where people compete about prizes that are external to the original game. When these activities turn into a professional level, the line between work and entertainment is blurred. Then, game accessibility becomes part of the larger community with further requirements for accessibility. Furthermore, game accessibility can also include board games and while the focus here is on computer games, the line is blurred with augmented or mixed reality technologies such as glasses or sensors that can provide user input or feedback with user adapted information. For details regarding recent development in the industry, the Game Accessibility Conference (gaconf.com) provides excellent updates of this two times per year. Video recordings of the conference are available for free online via the IGDA Game Accessibility SIG Youtube channel.[5]

Some Recent Game Accessibility Research

For the discussion, a few recent papers published during 2024 to time of this writing in April 2025 are briefly presented. Csontos and Heckl [1] present a clear method to visually present an analysis with a table view, based on the Xbox Accessibility Guidelines[6]. Larreina-Morales and Mangiron [2] surveyed 106 blind and low vision persons about audio descriptions in games, but also other desired options as well as current barriers. Screen reader support and audio descriptions were the two most wanted options. Westerholm, Tuuri, and Hassan [3] explores the use of music to convey information

---

[2] https://gameaccessibilityguidelines.com/.

[3] https://www.specialeffect.org.uk/how-we-can-help/eyemine.

[4] https://www.ucl.ac.uk/computer-science/collaborate/ucl-industry-exchange-network-ucl-ixn/touchless-computing-ucl-motioninput-3.

[5] https://www.youtube.com/channel/UCKWG26bBd7TOiaLtc_crqvw.

[6] https://learn.microsoft.com/en-us/gaming/accessibility/guidelines.

for improving accessibility for visually impaired and blind people, and found that user-informed music design was an improvement and combining thematic and adaptive music may be the best approach. Martinez, Froehlich, and Fogarty [4] present design recommendations supporting community-based approaches and customizable experiences for accessibility. The recommendations are based on 13 interviews with disabled people on their experiences, resources and strategies to overcome barriers in video games. Aljedaani et al. [5] conducted a survey with 73 deaf and hard-of-hearing persons regarding inconsistent captions in video games, and present caption best practices that are conspicuous, legible, unobtrusive, simple and space-efficient.

This small sample of recent research servers to show the diversity of research within game accessibility, ranging from various presentation methods with audio description [2], music [3] and captions [5], to design recommendations [4] and an evaluation method [1]. This diversity calls for more dialogue for how to collaborate which can be encouraged via the workshop.

2.2 A Brief Overview of Empowerment Through Generative AI

Generative AI and Social Value

The prevalence of AI in everyday work life has led to the creation of various sociotechnical systems. The value of AI should be understood in the context of the relationship between technology and society. However, ensuring that the adoption of AI systems supports, rather than undermines, social values remains a challenge [14]. There has been significant discussion surrounding ethical guidelines and strategies for responsible AI [11], as well as the sustainability of AI in promoting greater ecological integrity and social justice [16].

On the positive side, there has been extensive discussion on how AI can enrich social values. Research shows that the adoption of Large Language Models has great potential to enhance both efficiency and productivity [9], while image generation tools foster engagement among non-art professionals [23], enabling them to visually present ideas and boosting creativity in team collaborations [17]. Human-AI co-creation can also serve as a therapeutic tool to promote psychological well-being [12]. Furthermore, research highlights the significant potential of AI in improving global health, particularly in resource-poor settings [18].

Generative AI in Aesthetic Expression and Social Empowerment

Recent explorations of generative AI demonstrate its unique capacity to democratize aesthetic expression. For instance, AI enhances participatory design by improving accessibility and quality through two key mechanisms: lowering the participatory threshold and facilitating process execution, collaboration, and creation [8]. By integrating generative AI as a creativity support tool, stakeholders can engage in divergent thinking and visual expression more easily, as AI assists in translating text or parameters into visual outputs [15], providing real-time feedback, and inspiring idea generation [24]. These technological interventions offer new ways to redefine authorship as a distributed human-AI ecosystem.

Conflicts arise in multiple domains. Artists whose work was used without authorization for AI model training have been harmed by intellectual property infringement.

Many of them also believe that AI-generated content merely mimics human creativity, arguing that reliance on such tools diminishes the complexity of human innovation [13]. This issue is prominent across various fields. Recent research addresses ethical concerns in AI [20-22], including privacy, bias, accountability, transparency, safety, and societal impact. Additionally, some studies focus on the impact of AI on individuals, such as AI anxiety in learning, sociotechnical blindness, job displacement, and configuration challenges [19].

Ethical Considerations

Emerging technical frameworks are attempting to reconcile these tensions through value-sensitive design paradigms [7]. The development of attribution-aware diffusion models and ethical training datasets offers mechanisms to honor artistic labor while maintaining creative potential [6]. Additionally, human-in-the-loop validation systems are being prototyped to avoid aesthetic homogenization [10]. When combined with participatory governance models, these innovations suggest that generative AI can evolve into a dialogic medium, sustaining its aesthetic values while empowering communities to shape their own sociotechnical rule.

2.3 Workshop Format

This is a half-day workshop for the following activities, related to the goals:

- 45 min with pitch presentations: Authors present their papers in a fast-forward manner, each in 2–3 min
- 10-min break
- 90 min with two parallel round table discussions, one focusing on games, one focusing on gen AI and social value. Both groups are tasked with "identify gaps, opportunities, and challenges in game accessibility, inclusion, and empowerment through generative AI" but from respective perspectives.
- 5-min break
- 15-min presentations by a representative from each roundtable summarizing what gaps, opportunities, and challenges has been identified and what possible collaborations can be done.
- 15-min wrap-up on how to continue an academic forum format for advancing game accessibility and empowerment research until ICEC in Paris.
- Invited Speaker: Include a speaker related to the field.

As the point of having a workshop where some peer researchers perhaps meet for the first time to find possible collaborations in the future, the main part of the workshop are based on discussions. Also, recognizing the fields of game accessibility and empowerment through generative AI as research that require focus of their own, a main part of the the workshop is split into two parallel round table discussions. Also, to enable potential emerging collaborations across these partly overlapping fields, both the pitch presentations in the beginning and presentations from each roundtable are done with all participants. To move forward, the workshop ends with the wrap-up so we can make plans for the continuous effort about issues of both game accessibility and empowerment through generative AI until the next ICEC conference.

3   Expected Outcomes and Continued Work

Given the lively discussion and positive outcomes from ICEC 2024, this workshop hopefully provides a solid ground for advancing both fields and hopefully enable cross-collaborations between both fields as well, to be continued at ICEC 2025 in Paris.

Acknowledgments. We would like to thank ICEC for this opportunity to arrange this workshop.

Disclosure of Interests. The authors have no competing interests to declare that are relevant to the content of this article.

References

1. Csontos, B., Heckl, I.: The evolution of video game accessibility on Xbox consoles in the Far Cry game series. Univ. Access Inf. Soc. (2025)
2. Larreina-Morales, M.E., Mangiron, C.: Audio description in video games? Persons with visual disabilities weigh in. Univ. Access Inf. Soc. **23**(2), 577–588 (2024)
3. Westerholm, R., Tuuri, K., Hassan, L.: Not just atmosphere: game music design for accessible in-game information communication. In Proceedings of the 27th International Academic Mindtrek Conference, pp. 211–219. Association for Computing Machinery, Tampere (2024)
4. Martinez, J.J., Froehlich, J.E., Fogarty, J.: Playing on hard mode: accessibility, difficulty and joy in video game adoption for gamers with disabilities. In: Proceedings of the 2024 CHI Conference on Human Factors in Computing Systems, p. Article 524. Association for Computing Machinery: Honolulu (2024)
5. Aljedaani, W., et al.: Accessible gaming through better captions: a study on captions preferences and inclusivity of deaf and hard-of-hearing players. In: Proceedings of the 21st International Web for All Conference, pp. 75–86. Association for Computing Machinery, Singapore (2024)
6. Alacovska, A., Bissonnette, J.: Careful work: an ethics of care approach to contingent labour in the creative industries. J. Bus. Ethics **169**, 135–151 (2021)
7. Bergman, A.S., et al.: Guiding the release of safer e2e conversational ai through value sensitive design. In: Proceedings of the 23rd Annual Meeting of the Special Interest Group on Discourse and Dialogue. Association for Computational Linguistics (2022)
8. van den Broek, S., Sankaran, S., de Wit, J., de Rooij, A.: Exploring the supportive role of artificial intelligence in participatory design: a systematic review. In: Proceedings of the Participatory Design Conference 2024: Exploratory Papers and Workshops, vol. 2, pp. 37–44 (2024)
9. Bruscia, M., et al.: An overview on large language models across key domains: a systematic review. In: 2024 IEEE International Conference on Metrology for eXtended Reality, Artificial Intelligence and Neural Engineering (MetroXRAINE), pp. 125–130. IEEE (2024)
10. Chan, L., et al.: Investigating positive and negative qualities of human-in-the-loop optimization for designing interaction techniques. In: Proceedings of the 2022 CHI Conference on Human Factors in Computing Systems, pp. 1–14 (2022)
11. Contractor, D., et al.: Behavioral use licensing for responsible ai. In: Proceedings of the 2022 ACM Conference on Fairness, Accountability, and Transparency, pp. 778–788 (2022)
12. Du, X., An, P., Leung, J., Li, A., Chapman, L.E., Zhao, J.: Deepthink: designing and probing human-ai co-creation in digital art therapy. Int. J. Hum Comput Stud. **181**, 103139 (2024)

13. Jiang, H.H., et al.: Ai art and its impact on artists. In: Proceedings of the 2023 AAAI/ACM Conference on AI, Ethics, and Society, pp. 363–374 (2023)
14. Johnson, D.G., Verdicchio, M.: The sociotechnical entanglement of ai and values. AI Soc. 1–10 (2024)
15. Rafner, J., et al.: Crea.visions: a platform for casual co-creation with a purpose envisioning the future through human-ai collaboration with multiple stakeholders (2023)
16. Van Wynsberghe, A.: Sustainable Ai: Ai for sustainability and the sustainability of AI. AI Ethics 1(3), 213–218 (2021)
17. Verheijden, M.P., Funk, M.: Collaborative diffusion: boosting designerly cocreation with generative ai. In: Extended Abstracts of the 2023 CHI Conference on Human Factors in Computing Systems, pp. 1–8 (2023)
18. Wahl, B., Cossy-Gantner, A., Germann, S., Schwalbe, N.R.: Artificial intelligence (AI) and global health: how can AI contribute to health in resource-poor settings? BMJ Glob. Health 3(4), e000798 (2018)
19. Wang, Y.Y., Wang, Y.S.: Development and validation of an artificial intelligence anxiety scale: an initial application in predicting motivated learning behavior. Interact. Learn. Environ. 30(4), 619–634 (2022)
20. Xue, M., Yao, C., Hu, J., Feng, Y., Li, J., Hansen, P.: Aesthetics of connectivity for empowerment–considerations and challenges. In: Companion Publication of the 2024 ACM Designing Interactive Systems Conference, pp. 438–440 (2024)
21. Xue, M., Yao, C., Hu, J., Hu, Y., Lyu, H.: Aesthetics and empowerment. In: International Conference on Entertainment Computing, pp. 403–406. Springer, Heidelberg (2023)
22. Xue, M., Yao, C., Hu, J., Hu, Y., Lyu, H., Feng, Y.: Aesthetics and empowerment: exploring AI-driven creativity. In: International Conference on Entertainment Computing, pp. 316–320. Springer, Heidelberg (2024)
23. Zhang, C., et al.: Storydrawer: a child–ai collaborative drawing system to support children's creative visual storytelling. In: Proceedings of the 2022 CHI Conference on Human Factors in Computing Systems, pp. 1–15 (2022)
24. Zhang, G., Raina, A., Cagan, J., McComb, C.: A cautionary tale about the impact of AI on human design teams. Des. Stud. 72, 100990 (2021)

Beyond Scripts: Designing and Evaluating GenAI-Based NPCs in Video Games

Nima Zargham$^{(\boxtimes)}$ ⓘ, Leon Tristan Dratzidis ⓘ, Mehrdad Bahrini ⓘ,
Rachel Ringe ⓘ, Lisa Hesselbarth ⓘ, and Rainer Malaka ⓘ

Digital Media Lab, Universtiy of Bremen, Bremen, Germany
{zargham,dratzidis,mbahrini,rringe,lihe,malaka}@uni-bremen.de

Abstract. The rise of large language models (LLMs) and generative AI (GenAI) has transformed game development by enabling game designers new ways to increase player engagement and interaction. One significant application is the creation of NPCs capable of dynamic, unscripted communication. While multiplayer games thrive on social engagement, single-player experiences often suffer from pre-scripted NPC interactions. However, the challenges and implications of integrating GenAI-based NPCs into games remain largely unexplored. This workshop brings together researchers and game developers to discuss the potential and limitations of GenAI-based NPCs, their impact on player experience, and the social and ethical concerns they raise. By facilitating dialogue on best practices and research directions, we aim to initiate discussion on the next generation of intelligent, socially responsive NPCs that enhance immersion and engagement in gaming.

Keywords: NPC Communication · Generative AI · Large Language Models · Natural Language Interaction

1 Motivation and Goals

The advancement of large language models (LLMs) and generative AI (GenAI) has opened new possibilities for game development [8,18,30]. These technologies are increasingly being used for procedural content generation (PCG) [24], map and level design [31], narrative development [20], and quest descriptions [34]. Additionally, researchers have explored the use of LLMs to design NPCs that can engage in more dynamic and adaptive interactions with players [17,27,36].

As the gaming industry evolves to meet increasing consumer demand, video games strive to deliver more immersive experiences [9,22]. A key trend is the shift toward natural interactions [23], with technologies like virtual reality (VR) bringing players closer to seamless engagement with game environments. Social interaction is another crucial factor influencing immersion [21,48]. Particularly in multiplayer games, natural language communication fosters community, engagement, and enjoyment [10,11]. In contrast, single-player games often lack meaningful social interaction, limiting players to scripted exchanges with NPCs, typically through dialogue trees [41]. These static interactions lack the dynamism

Published by Springer Nature Switzerland AG 2025
R. Yamanishi et al. (Eds.): ICEC 2025 Workshops, LNCS 15935, pp. 24–33, 2025.
https://doi.org/10.1007/978-3-032-02534-0_5

and responsiveness of real-time human conversations [37], making single-player experiences feel predictable [10]. Over time, this reduces replay value and can lead to player disengagement [7]. While multiplayer games facilitate camaraderie and teamwork through player interaction [13,14], studies suggest similar social bonds emerge from engaging NPC interactions [41]. Research shows that when people interact with computers through natural language, they tend to apply social expectations, responding as if communicating with a human [26,29].

Recent research has explored the use of GenAI to create NPCs capable of dynamic, unscripted dialogue. Unlike traditional pre-scripted options, these GenAI-based NPCs allow players to engage in freeform conversations, generating more varied and responsive interactions. Wan et al. [35] evaluated LLM-based NPCs in the social VR platform VRChat [33], focusing on optimizing contextual responses. Their study found that GenAI-based NPCs could deliver relevant dialogue synchronized with facial expressions and gestures. Similarly, Volum et al. [32] examined player interactions with a GenAI-based NPC in Minecraft, revealing that while players enjoyed the experience, they encountered issues with out-of-character and irrelevant responses that sometimes disrupted immersion. Conversational tools like InWorld AI [19] and Convai [12] enable developers to design and manage AI-powered NPCs for games, virtual worlds, and immersive environments. Despite their potential, GenAI-based NPCs also raise several concerns. One issue raised is the potential for players to use inappropriate or abusive language without real-world consequences [37]. Another concern is the risk of increased social isolation caused by excessive play, as the heightened immersion and interactions with the dynamic NPCs may negatively impact players' real-world social interactions [37]. As AI technology advances, GenAI-powered agents will become increasingly prevalent in gaming [28]. As these systems continue to evolve, it is crucial to assess their integration to understand both the benefits and challenges they present. This includes examining how players perceive interactions with AI-based NPCs and identifying potential social and ethical concerns that may arise from their use.

This full-day workshop aims to bring together researchers and developers to critically discuss the future of NPC design and interactions, with a focus on GenAI-based characters, their potential, and their challenges. We aim to address how AI advancements are shaping the future of NPC design, which factors are essential for creating dynamic NPCs, and how their integration can enhance player experience. The workshop will also address the ethical and social implications of AI-based NPCs, aiming to establish guidelines for fostering healthy and meaningful player-NPC interactions. Ultimately, we seek to build a community of researchers and practitioners dedicated to shaping the future of dynamic NPCs in game development.

2   Organisers

This workshop is organized by a team of experienced researchers with expertise spanning diverse fields aligned with our objectives. The organizers have a strong record of publications in areas such as game user research [2–5,37,41,42,44,45] and conversational user interfaces [1,6,38–40,46,47]. We aim to foster collaboration among participants from various backgrounds and promote transdisciplinary innovation. Multiple successful workshops were held between the organizers at HCI conferences, such as HRI'23 [25], CUI'23 [1], CUI'24 [16], MUM'24 [43], and CHI'24 [15].

Nima Zargham is a postdoctoral researcher in the Digital Media Lab at the University of Bremen. His research focuses on human-centered approaches for designing speech-based systems that elicit desirable user experiences. Nima has previously organized CUI-related workshops at notable conferences such as ACM/IEEE HRI 2023, ACM CUI 2023–2024, MUM 2024, and ACM CHI 24. Additionally, he served as a local chair at the ACM CHI-PLAY 2022 conference.

Leon Tristan Dratzidis is a PhD student in the Digital Media Lab at the University of Bremen. In his research, he investigates the dynamic interplay between player agency and AI agency in interactive digital environments, focusing on how factors such as game mechanics, narrative structures, and autonomous agent behaviors shape user experience.

Mehrdad Bahrini is a postdoctoral researcher in the Digital Media Lab at the University of Bremen. His research explores usable security and privacy, focusing on how motivation, ability, and behavioral triggers influence user behavior in mobile and ubiquitous applications. He develops user-centered security solutions by integrating psychological principles. His work leverages serious games, gamification, interactive visualizations, and AR interfaces to enhance user engagement with privacy and security tasks.

Rachel Ringe is a PhD student in the Digital Media Lab at the University of Bremen. Her research examines human-robot interaction in household settings, focusing on how factors like appearance and behavior impact the interaction. Due to her research being conducted mostly in virtual environments, her work also incorporates examinations of VR interfaces and interactions as well as gamification approaches.

Lisa Hesselbarth is a PhD student in the Digital Media Lab at the University of Bremen. Her research focuses on empowering users' creativity in the interaction with novel technologies such as GenAI. Her work focuses on haptic and tangible interactions to enhance creative processes, motivation, control, and engagement with new user interfaces.

Rainer Malaka is a professor of Digital Media at the University of Bremen. His research focus is on multi-modal interaction, language understanding, entertainment computing, and artificial intelligence. He was a General Chair at the ACM CHI PLAY 2022, the IFIP Conference on Entertainment Computing 2012, and the German HCI conference MuC 2013.

3   Schedule and Workshop Activities

We aim to organize this workshop as a full-day event. The tentative schedule and activities are outlined below:

- **Welcome & Introduction (30 min):** We will begin with brief introductions from the organizers and participants, outlining the workshop's objectives and providing an overview of the day's agenda.
- **Presentations (30 min):** Each participant will have 3–5 min to introduce themselves and present their accepted paper. This will allow everyone to share their background, research focus, and key insights from their work.
- **GenAI-Based NPCs Demonstration (30 min):** The organizers will showcase selected games and prototypes featuring GenAI-based NPCs and highlight their interactions and key design choices. This will be followed by an open discussion where participants can share insights, critique the designs, and explore their impact on player experience.
- **Coffee Break (30 min)**
- **Prototype Activity (90 min):** Participants will be divided into small groups, each guided by a facilitator. Each group will be assigned a specific game genre and NPC role, such as a quest-giving mentor in an open-world RPG, a rival in a competitive shooter, or a shopkeeper in a survival game. The task begins with defining the core characteristics of the NPC, including their personality traits, background, and narrative function, while considering how the NPC's behavior should dynamically adapt to player interactions. Groups will also decide how the NPC communicates (e.g., voice or text). With support from the organizers, participants will prototype their NPCs using Unity[1]. Pre-designed scenes will be provided, allowing groups to integrate and test their NPCs in a relevant game environment. Once the NPCs are placed within these scenes, participants from other groups will interact with them and give initial feedback. At the end of the session, each group will present their designed NPC, explaining their design rationale. The broader audience will provide feedback and discuss potential refinements or alternative approaches.
- **Lunch (90 min)**
- **Concluding the Prototyping & NPC Evaluation (30 min):** Each group will refine their NPCs based on initial feedback and address design or interaction issues identified during the first round of testing. This may include adjusting dialogue flow, modifying NPC behaviors, or fine-tuning interaction mechanics. Following these refinements, groups will briefly reflect on their design choices, discussing what worked well, what challenges they encountered, and how they addressed them.
- **Keynote & Discussion (60 min):** Our keynote will be delivered by **Dr. Maximilian A. Friehs**. He is an Assistant Professor of the Psychology of Conflict, Risk, and Safety at the University of Twente, exploring the neurophysiological foundations of cognitive control, examining how motivation

---

[1] https://unity3d.com/unity.

influences performance and how games shape motivation. His current research investigates the impact of virtual agents on human experiences and behavior, investigating how certain aspects of virtual agents influence human experiences and behavior, whether we can elicit "realistic" behaviors and experiences in a game, and how we can increase immersion in virtual environments. He has published several papers on generative AI in NPC design with a focus on the social side of interacting with such agents.

- **Coffee Break (30 min)**
- **Closing (60 min):** The workshop will conclude with a summary of key insights, followed by a collaborative reflection where participants and organizers identify concrete research topics and potential outcomes. The session will also explore future research directions and strategies for upcoming venues and workshops, incorporating participant feedback.

4   Format and Advertisement

This workshop seeks to bring together individuals from academia and industry to enable cross-disciplinary dialogue on GenAI-based NPCs. To reach potential participants, we will distribute a Call for Participation through multiple channels, including social media platforms (e.g., Facebook and LinkedIn) and relevant mailing lists. Additionally, we will extend direct invitations to researchers with prior publications in related fields. The workshop will be held exclusively in person, with an expected attendance of 7 to 15 participants and 3 to 5 position paper submissions. A dedicated workshop website (https://dml.uni-bremen.de/alive-characters) will provide information on the call, key dates, and participation details. Accepted submissions will be posted on the website before the workshop and archived afterward for reference. Participants are invited to submit position papers (2–4 pages) presenting their research, innovative ideas, or perspectives on the design and evaluation of GenAI-based NPCs in video games. We welcome submissions on ongoing research, preliminary results for discussion, methodological approaches, and design insights. Each submission will undergo independent review by at least two workshop organizers before acceptance. Additionally, we encourage expressions of interest from individuals who may not have formal papers but wish to contribute. These statements should outline relevant experience, perspectives, or ideas related to the workshop theme.

5   Inclusion and Accessibility

We are committed to fostering an inclusive and accessible environment for all attendees and will work closely with the conference organizers to ensure this. We will proactively address participants' identified accessibility needs and provide the necessary resources to support their engagement. Drawing from our experience organizing previous conferences and workshops, we strive to create a space where all participants are valued as equal contributors to the discussion. Additionally, we aim to encourage meaningful connections by facilitating structured breakout sessions and mentorship opportunities and create spaces for cross-disciplinary collaboration and learning.

6   Post-workshop Plans

The primary goal of this workshop is to promote collaboration among participants from diverse backgrounds who share an interest in designing and evaluating GenAI-based NPCs. To ensure broad dissemination, all accepted participant submissions will be published on the workshop website. Additionally, the participants will be encouraged to publish their position papers on platforms such as $arXiv$[2] or $ceur\text{-}ws$[3]. Additionally, we aim to synthesize key workshop findings into a refined publication for a relevant venue, such as IFIP ICEC 2026. Key discussion points and insights will be documented on an open online platform during and after the workshop to enable continued engagement. Participants will also be encouraged to explore future collaborative projects inspired by the discussions. To sustain community engagement beyond the workshop, we will implement a long-term strategy using social media, mailing lists, and other platforms to keep participants connected and informed about developments in the topic.

Acknowledgments. This work was partially funded by Klaus Tschira Foundation, the FET-Open Project 951846 "MUHAI – Meaning and Understanding for Human-centric AI" funded by the EU program Horizon 2020, as well as the German Research Foundation DFG as part of Collaborative Research Center (Sonderforschungsbereich) 1320 "EASE – Everyday Activity Science and Engineering", University of Bremen (http://www.ease-crc.org/).

References

1. Avanesi, V., et al.: From C-3PO to HAL: opening the discourse about the dark side of multi-modal social agents. In: Proceedings of the 5th International Conference on Conversational User Interfaces, CUI 2023. Association for Computing Machinery, New York (2023). https://doi.org/10.1145/3571884.3597441
2. Bahrini, M., Volkmar, G., Schmutte, J., Wenig, N., Sohr, K., Malaka, R.: Make my phone secure! Using gamification for mobile security settings. In: Proceedings of Mensch Und Computer 2019, MuC 2019, pp. 299–308. Association for Computing Machinery, New York (2019). https://doi.org/10.1145/3340764.3340775
3. Bahrini, M., Weglewski, J., Sohr, K., Malaka, R.: Empowering user security awareness and risk assessment within gamified smartphone environment. In: Figueroa, P., Di Iorio, A., Guzman del Rio, D., Gonzalez Clua, E.W., Cuevas Rodriguez, L. (eds.) ICEC 2024. LNCS, vol. 15192, pp. 16–34. Springer, Cham (2025). https://doi.org/10.1007/978-3-031-74353-5_2

---

[2] https://arxiv.org/.
[3] https://ceur-ws.org/.

4. Bahrini, M., Zargham, N., Pfau, J., Lemke, S., Sohr, K., Malaka, R.: Enhancing game-based learning through infographics in the context of smart home security. In: Nunes, N.J., Ma, L., Wang, M., Correia, N., Pan, Z. (eds.) ICEC 2020. LNCS, vol. 12523, pp. 18–36. Springer, Cham (2020). https://doi.org/10.1007/978-3-030-65736-9_2

5. Bahrini, M., Zargham, N., Pfau, J., Lemke, S., Sohr, K., Malaka, R.: Good vs. evil: investigating the effect of game premise in a smart home security educational game. In: Extended Abstracts of the 2020 Annual Symposium on Computer-Human Interaction in Play, CHI PLAY 2020, pp. 182–187. Association for Computing Machinery, New York (2020). https://doi.org/10.1145/3383668.3419887

6. Bonfert, M., Zargham, N., Saade, F., Porzel, R., Malaka, R.: An evaluation of visual embodiment for voice assistants on smart displays. In: CUI 2021-3rd Conference on Conversational User Interfaces, pp. 1–11. ACM, New York (2021)

7. Bowey, J.T., Friehs, M.A., Mandryk, R.L.: Red or blue pill: fostering identification and transportation through dialogue choices in RPGs. In: Proceedings of the 14th International Conference on the Foundations of Digital Games, FDG 2019. Association for Computing Machinery, New York (2019). https://doi.org/10.1145/3337722.3337734

8. Bubeck, S., et al.: Sparks of artificial general intelligence: early experiments with GPT-4 (2023)

9. Cairns, P., Cox, A., Nordin, A.I.: Immersion in Digital Games: Review of Gaming Experience Research, chap. 12, pp. 337–361. Wiley, Hoboken (2014). https://doi.org/10.1002/9781118796443.ch12

10. Chen, V.H.-H., Duh, H.B.-L., Phuah, P.S.K., Lam, D.Z.Y.: Enjoyment or engagement? Role of social interaction in playing massively mulitplayer online role-playing games (MMORPGS). In: Harper, R., Rauterberg, M., Combetto, M. (eds.) ICEC 2006. LNCS, vol. 4161, pp. 262–267. Springer, Heidelberg (2006). https://doi.org/10.1007/11872320_31

11. Cole, H., Griffiths, M.D.: Social interactions in massively multiplayer online role-playing gamers. Cyberpsychol. Behav. **10**(4), 575–583 (2007). https://doi.org/10.1089/cpb.2007.9988. pMID: 17711367

12. Convai Inc.: Convai. https://convai.com/. Accessed 20 Jan 2025

13. Depping, A.E., Johanson, C., Mandryk, R.L.: Designing for friendship: modeling properties of play, in-game social capital, and psychological well-being. In: Proceedings of the 2018 Annual Symposium on Computer-Human Interaction in Play, CHI PLAY 2018, pp. 87–100. Association for Computing Machinery, New York (2018). https://doi.org/10.1145/3242671.3242702

14. Depping, A.E., Mandryk, R.L.: Cooperation and interdependence: how multiplayer games increase social closeness. In: Proceedings of the Annual Symposium on Computer-Human Interaction in Play, CHI PLAY 2017, pp. 449–461. Association for Computing Machinery, New York (2017). https://doi.org/10.1145/3116595.3116639

15. Desai, S., et al.: CUI@CHI 2024: building trust in CUIS—from design to deployment. In: Extended Abstracts of the CHI Conference on Human Factors in Computing Systems, CHI EA 2024. Association for Computing Machinery, New York (2024). https://doi.org/10.1145/3613905.3636287

16. Dubiel, M., Desai, S., Zargham, N., Schmitt, A.: Voicecraft: designing task-specific voice assistant personas. In: Proceedings of the 6th ACM Conference on Conversational User Interfaces, CUI 2024. Association for Computing Machinery, New York (2024). https://doi.org/10.1145/3640794.3670000

17. Gao, Q.C., Emami, A.: The Turing quest: can transformers make good NPCs? In: Padmakumar, V., Vallejo, G., Fu, Y. (eds.) Proceedings of the 61st Annual Meeting of the Association for Computational Linguistics (Volume 4: Student Research Workshop), Toronto, Canada, pp. 93–103. Association for Computational Linguistics (2023). https://doi.org/10.18653/v1/2023.acl-srw.17

18. Garcia-Pi, B., et al.: AllyChat: developing a VR conversational AI agent using few-shot learning to support individuals with intellectual disabilities. In: Abdelnour Nocera, J., Kristín Lárusdóttir, M., Petrie, H., Piccinno, A., Winckler, M. (eds.) INTERACT 2023. LNCS, vol. 14145, pp. 402–407. Springer, Cham (2023). https://doi.org/10.1007/978-3-031-42293-5_43

19. InWorld AI Inc.: InWorld AI. https://inworld.ai/. Accessed 20 Jan 2025

20. Kumaran, V., Rowe, J., Mott, B., Lester, J.: SceneCraft: automating interactive narrative scene generation in digital games with large language models. In: Proceedings of the AAAI Conference on Artificial Intelligence and Interactive Digital Entertainment, vol. 19, pp. 86–96 (2023)

21. Lee, K.M., Peng, W., Jin, S.A., Yan, C.: Can robots manifest personality?: An empirical test of personality recognition, social responses, and social presence in human-robot interaction. J. Commun. **56**(4), 754–772 (2006)

22. Leroy, R.: Immersion, flow and usability in video games. In: Extended Abstracts of the 2021 CHI Conference on Human Factors in Computing Systems, CHI EA 2021. Association for Computing Machinery, New York (2021). https://doi.org/10.1145/3411763.3451514

23. Malaka, R., et al.: Using natural user interfaces for previsualization. EAI Endorsed Trans. Creat. Technol. **8**(26) (2021)

24. Maleki, M.F., Zhao, R.: Procedural content generation in games: a survey with insights on emerging LLM integration. In: Proceedings of the AAAI Conference on Artificial Intelligence and Interactive Digital Entertainment, vol. 20, pp. 167–178 (2024)

25. McMillan, D., et al.: Human-robot conversational interaction (HRCI). In: Companion of the 2023 ACM/IEEE International Conference on Human-Robot Interaction, HRI 2023, pp. 923–925. Association for Computing Machinery, New York (2023). https://doi.org/10.1145/3568294.3579954

26. Nass, C.I., Brave, S.: Wired for Speech: How Voice Activates and Advances the Human-Computer Relationship. MIT Press, Cambridge (2005)

27. Park, J.S., O'Brien, J., Cai, C.J., Morris, M.R., Liang, P., Bernstein, M.S.: Generative agents: interactive simulacra of human behavior. In: Proceedings of the 36th Annual ACM Symposium on User Interface Software and Technology, UIST 2023. Association for Computing Machinery, New York (2023). https://doi.org/10.1145/3586183.3606763

28. Rao, S., et al.: Collaborative quest completion with LLM-driven non-player characters in minecraft (2024). https://arxiv.org/abs/2407.03460

29. Shani, C., Libov, A., Tolmach, S., Lewin-Eytan, L., Maarek, Y., Shahaf, D.: "Alexa, do you want to build a snowman?" characterizing playful requests to conversational agents. In: Extended Abstracts of the 2022 CHI Conference on Human Factors in Computing Systems, CHI EA 2022. Association for Computing Machinery, New York (2022). https://doi.org/10.1145/3491101.3519870

30. Shoa, A., Oliva, R., Slater, M., Friedman, D.: Sushi with Einstein: enhancing hybrid live events with LLM-based virtual humans. In: Proceedings of the 23rd ACM International Conference on Intelligent Virtual Agents, IVA 2023. Association for Computing Machinery, New York (2023). https://doi.org/10.1145/3570945.3607317

31. Todd, G., Earle, S., Nasir, M.U., Green, M.C., Togelius, J.: Level generation through large language models. In: Proceedings of the 18th International Conference on the Foundations of Digital Games, FDG 2023. Association for Computing Machinery, New York (2023). https://doi.org/10.1145/3582437.3587211

32. Volum, R., et al.: Craft an iron sword: dynamically generating interactive game characters by prompting large language models tuned on code. In: Côté, M.A., Yuan, X., Ammanabrolu, P. (eds.) Proceedings of the 3rd Wordplay: When Language Meets Games Workshop (Wordplay 2022), Seattle, United States, pp. 25–43. Association for Computational Linguistics (2022). https://doi.org/10.18653/v1/2022.wordplay-1.3

33. VRChat Inc.: VRChat. https://hello.vrchat.com/. Accessed 20 Jan 2025

34. Värtinen, S., Hämäläinen, P., Guckelsberger, C.: Generating role-playing game quests with GPT language models. IEEE Trans. Games **16**(1), 127–139 (2024). https://doi.org/10.1109/TG.2022.3228480

35. Wan, H., Zhang, J., Suria, A.A., Yao, B., Wang, D., Coady, Y., Prpa, M.: Building LLM-based AI agents in social virtual reality. In: Extended Abstracts of the CHI Conference on Human Factors in Computing Systems, CHI EA 2024. Association for Computing Machinery, New York (2024). https://doi.org/10.1145/3613905.3651026

36. Wang, G., et al.: Voyager: an open-ended embodied agent with large language models (2023). https://arxiv.org/abs/2305.16291

37. Zargham, N., et al.: Let's talk games: an expert exploration of speech interaction with NPCs. Int. J. Hum.–Comput. Interact. **0**(0), 1–21 (2024). https://doi.org/10.1080/10447318.2024.2338666

38. Zargham, N., Alexandrovsky, D., Erich, J., Wenig, N., Malaka, R.: "I want it that way": exploring users' customization and personalization preferences for home assistants. In: Extended Abstracts of the 2022 CHI Conference on Human Factors in Computing Systems, CHI EA 2022. Association for Computing Machinery, New York (2022). https://doi.org/10.1145/3491101.3519843

39. Zargham, N., Bahrini, M., Volkmar, G., Wenig, D., Sohr, K., Malaka, R.: What could go wrong? Raising mobile privacy and security awareness through a decision-making game. In: Extended Abstracts of the Annual Symposium on Computer-Human Interaction in Play Companion Extended Abstracts, CHI PLAY 2019 Extended Abstracts, pp. 805–812. Association for Computing Machinery, New York (2019). https://doi.org/10.1145/3341215.3356273

40. Zargham, N., Bonfert, M., Porzel, R., Doring, T., Malaka, R.: Multi-agent voice assistants: an investigation of user experience. In: 20th International Conference on Mobile and Ubiquitous Multimedia, MUM 2021, pp. 98–107. Association for Computing Machinery, New York (2021). https://doi.org/10.1145/3490632.3490662

41. Zargham, N., Bonfert, M., Volkmar, G., Porzel, R., Malaka, R.: Smells like team spirit: investigating the player experience with multiple interlocutors in a VR game. In: Extended Abstracts of the 2020 Annual Symposium on Computer-Human Interaction in Play, CHI PLAY 2020, pp. 408–412. Association for Computing Machinery, New York (2020). https://doi.org/10.1145/3383668.3419884

42. Zargham, N., Dratzidis, L.T., Alexandrovsky, D., Friehs, M.A., Malaka, R.: Gaming with etiquette: exploring courtesy as a game mechanic in speech-based games. Int. J. Hum.-Comput. Interact., 1–19 (2024). https://doi.org/10.1080/10447318.2024.2387901

43. Zargham, N., Dubiel, M., Desai, S., Mildner, T., Belz, H.J.: Designing AI person-alities: enhancing human-agent interaction through thoughtful persona design. In: Proceedings of the International Conference on Mobile and Ubiquitous Multimedia, MUM 2024, pp. 490–494. Association for Computing Machinery, New York (2024). https://doi.org/10.1145/3701571.3701608

44. Zargham, N., Fetni, M.L., Spillner, L., Muender, T., Malaka, R.: "I know what you mean": context-aware recognition to enhance speech-based games. In: Proceedings of the CHI Conference on Human Factors in Computing Systems, CHI 2024. Association for Computing Machinery, New York (2024). https://doi.org/10.1145/3613904.3642426

45. Zargham, N., Pfau, J., Schnackenberg, T., Malaka, R.: "I didn't catch that, but i'll try my best": anticipatory error handling in a voice controlled game. In: Proceedings of the 2022 CHI Conference on Human Factors in Computing Systems, CHI 2022. Association for Computing Machinery, New York (2022). https://doi.org/10.1145/3491102.3502115

46. Zargham, N., Reicherts, L., Avanesi, V., Rogers, Y., Malaka, R.: Tickling proactivity: exploring the use of humor in proactive voice assistants. In: Proceedings of the 22nd International Conference on Mobile and Ubiquitous Multimedia, MUM 2023, pp. 294–320. Association for Computing Machinery, New York (2023). https://doi.org/10.1145/3626705.3627777

47. Zargham, N., et al.: Understanding circumstances for desirable proactive behaviour of voice assistants: the proactivity dilemma. In: Proceedings of the 4th Conference on Conversational User Interfaces, CUI 2022. Association for Computing Machinery, New York (2022). https://doi.org/10.1145/3543829.3543834

48. Zhao, R., Wang, K., Divekar, R., Rouhani, R., Su, H., Ji, Q.: An immersive system with multi-modal human-computer interaction. In: 2018 13th IEEE International Conference on Automatic Face & Gesture Recognition (FG 2018), pp. 517–524. IEEE, New York (2018)

AERS2025: Accessibility and Empowerment Research Summit

Enhancing Biofeedback Interventions for Depression and Anxiety Through Entertainment Computing: A Systematic Review

Tasnim Afra⬤, Mengru Xue(✉)⬤, and Minhazul Islam⬤

Ningbo Global Innovation Center, Zhejiang University, Ningbo, China
mengruxue@zju.edu.cn

Abstract. Depression and anxiety are prevalent mental health disorders with complex psychological and physiological symptoms. Biofeedback interventions provide real-time physiological feedback and show promise as non-pharmacological treatments. Recent advances in entertainment computing, such as virtual reality (VR), artificial intelligence (AI), wearables, and gamification, offer new opportunities to enhance biofeedback outside clinical settings. This systematic review examines 45 peer-reviewed studies from 2019 to 2025, identified via PubMed, IEEE Xplore, ACM, Embase, and Cochrane Library, following PRISMA guidelines. Findings highlight neurofeedback, heart rate variability (HRV), and visual feedback as effective in improving brain modulation and emotional regulation. However, challenges remain in usability, personalization, and real-world integration. We recommend that future research focus on adaptive, user-centered designs leveraging wearable, VR, and AI technologies. This review provides an updated perspective on the evolving role of biofeedback interventions in managing depression and anxiety, emphasizing human-computer interaction considerations.

Keywords: Biofeedback · Depression · Anxiety · Virtual Reality (VR) · Human Computer Interaction (HCI)

1 Introduction

Depression and anxiety are among the most prevalent mental health disorders worldwide, affecting millions across all age groups. Despite the availability of effective treatments, only about 27.6% of individuals with anxiety disorders receive care, and in low- and middle-income countries, 75% of people with depression remain untreated [1,2]. This highlights an urgent need for scalable, accessible, and non-pharmacological interventions.

Internet-based psychological interventions (ICBT) have improved accessibility but often require high user motivation and engagement, which can be challenging for those suffering from these disorders [3]. This underscores the potential of technology-enhanced psychological interventions and alternative therapeutic modalities. Biofeedback is a promising non-invasive approach that helps

R. Yamanishi et al. (Eds.): ICEC 2025 Workshops, LNCS 15935, pp. 37–51, 2025.
https://doi.org/10.1007/978-3-032-02534-0_6

individuals monitor and regulate physiological responses, thereby reducing discomfort and improving mental health [8,9]. By providing real-time feedback on bodily functions, biofeedback empowers users to consciously control autonomic nervous system reactions and has been effectively combined with other therapies. Recent advances in entertainment computing technologies—such as wearable devices, artificial intelligence (AI), virtual reality (VR), and games—have transformed mental health care by enabling real-time monitoring, personalized interventions, and greater portability beyond clinical settings [4,5]. These innovations have enhanced the usability and scalability of biofeedback interventions for depression and anxiety. Notably, VR-enhanced biofeedback, EEG neurofeedback, and wearable sensors have shown promise in improving anxiety and mindfulness outcomes [11,47]. However, existing reviews predominantly focus on biofeedback's medical applications for conditions like hypertension and chronic pain, often overlooking its specific effectiveness for depression and anxiety, and prior studies lack detailed analysis of human-computer interaction (HCI) factors and comparative benefits over other therapies [8,53].

By presenting current research gaps and trends in biofeedback applications for depression and anxiety, this review aims to address these gaps by thoroughly evaluating biofeedback's effectiveness in treating depression and anxiety. We defined our research questions as follows:

RQ1: What are the most prevalent biofeedback techniques used in the treatment of depression and anxiety (2019–2025)?

RQ2: How are entertainment computing technologies like virtual reality(VR), games, artificial intelligence (AI), and wearable devices currently being integrated with specific biofeedback interventions for treating depression and anxiety?

2   Methodology

2.1   Search Strategies and Sources of Data

Five well-known electronic databases—PubMed, IEEE Xplore, ACM Digital Library, Embase, and the Cochrane Library were thoroughly searched to ensure the identification of relevant studies. The main goal was to search papers that covered two important subjects: "Depression or Anxiety" and "Biofeedback". Medical Subject Headings (MeSH) terms, spelling variations, and synonyms were used in particular search strategies for every database to improve the retrieval of relevant studies.

1. Biofeedback: (biofeedback OR "biofeedback" OR "neurofeedback" OR "Brainwave Biofeedback" OR "augmented feedback" OR "sensory feedback" OR "sensory augmentation" OR "electromyography Feedback" OR "auditory feedback" OR "audio feedback" OR "audio-feedback" OR "visual feedback" OR "audiovisual feedback" OR "somatosensory feedback" OR "tactile feedback" OR "vibrotactile feedback" OR "vibratory feedback" OR "multimodal feedback" OR "EEG biofeedback" OR "EMG biofeedback" OR "ECG

biofeedback" OR "EDA biofeedback" OR "HRV biofeedback" OR "Thermal feedback" OR "Respiratory feedback" OR "peripheral feedback" OR "cognitive behavioral therapy" OR "CBT").

2. Depression or Anxiety: ("anxiety" OR "anxious" OR "depression" OR "depressed" OR "depressive" OR "major depressive disorder" OR "MDD" OR "emotional disorder" OR "mood disorders" OR "dysthymia").

3. Combined search strategy: (1 AND 2).

2.2 Selection Criteria

This review defines biofeedback as real-time monitoring of physiological activity used to manage depression or anxiety symptoms. Included studies met the following criteria: involved biofeedback interventions, assessed depression or anxiety symptoms, used human data, were published in English, and appeared between January 2019 and March 2025. Excluded were non-biofeedback studies, non-human data, non-English articles, reviews, books, commentaries, workshops, panels, mock-ups, and studies outside the date range. Table 1 summarizes these criteria.

Table 1. Article Selection Criteria

Inclusion Criteria	Exclusion Criteria
Biofeedback intervention	No biofeedback involvement
Measures depression or anxiety symptoms	Reviews, books, commentaries
Human data	Workshops, panels, mock-ups
English language	Non-English articles
Published Jan 2019–Mar 2025	Outside date range

2.3 The Selection Procedure Process and Search Results

The study selection process criteria were followed by the preferred reporting items for systematic reviews and meta-analyses (PRISMA), as shown in Fig. 1. Two independent reviewers (TA and MX) screened the titles and abstracts of the remaining articles after removing duplicates. After reading through the full texts, the two reviewers again select which articles to include and exclude according to the predefined criteria. A total of 360 articles from different sources, covering PubMed (192), IEEE Xplore (43), ACM Digital Library (48), Embase (26), and the Cochrane Library (51) were identified in the initial database search. Out of them, 322 articles were evaluated for full-text eligibility, with one item not being able to be collected. After the exclusion criteria were carefully followed, 279 items were excluded for different reasons: out of the total, 137 did not primarily address depression or biofeedback; 81 belonged to other areas of expertise; 4 were work in

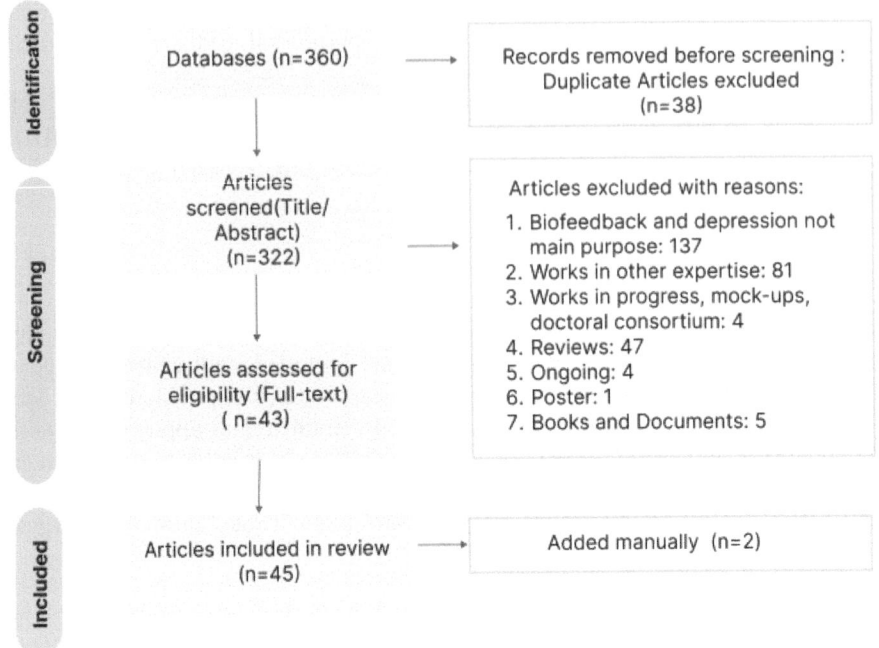

Fig. 1. PRISMA flowchart of literature search results

progress, mock-ups, or works in progress; 47 were reviews; 4 ongoing studies; 1 poster; and 5 books and documents. A total of 45 articles were included in the final review.

3   Results

3.1   RQ1: What are the Most Prevalent Biofeedback Techniques Used in the Treatment of Depression and Anxiety (2019–2025)?

Neurofeedback is among the most widely used biofeedback modalities, primarily involving EEG and fMRI-based approaches that train users to regulate brain activity via real-time feedback. EEG neurofeedback commonly employs scalp electrodes with visual or auditory cues [16,34]. fMRI neurofeedback studies target overlapping brain networks implicated in depression, such as the default mode, central executive, and saliency networks—using similar equipment and software (e.g., Siemens 3T MRI, FRIEND, Turbo BrainVoyager) [19,32,33,37]. Due to this methodological overlap, these studies should be interpreted collectively as evidence supporting general fMRI neurofeedback efficacy rather than independent validations. Additionally, swLORETA Z-score neurofeedback shows promise for comorbid anxiety and depression [34].

Heart Rate Variability (HRV) biofeedback enables autonomic regulation through guided breathing exercises, typically using PPG or ECG sensors integrated into wearables (e.g., Polar H10, NeXus-4) or mobile apps like

Elite HRV [31,39,41]. Studies across diverse populations, including VR-induced communication anxiety [17], major depressive disorder (MDD) patients [24], and healthcare workers [41] demonstrate consistent symptom reductions. Similar devices and protocols across these studies suggest a shared methodological framework.

Visual feedback, often embedded in VR environments, integrates physiological signals such as respiration, heart rate, and EEG to enhance engagement and emotional regulation [6,55]. Interventions like SeekingHeart and Emoregulator share common platforms (Unity3D, EEG headsets) and should be viewed as complementary explorations of a unified technological approach. Other studies use VR to visualize respiratory biofeedback [14] or combine visual-auditory feedback for anxiety reduction [20].

Integration of Biofeedback and Psychological Interventions highlights the synergistic potential for treating depression and anxiety. For example, one study found that both a neurofeedback-based videogame (MindLight) and online CBT significantly reduced anxiety symptoms in youth [56]. Another reported that patients with dyssynergic defecation receiving combined biofeedback therapy (BFT) and CBT showed greater improvements in anxiety, depression, and quality of life compared to BFT or standard care alone [57]. Significant reductions in depressive symptoms were observed following both real-time fMRI neurofeedback and CBT [58]. Additionally, neurofeedback and CBT were both effective for generalized anxiety disorder in children and youth, with neurofeedback providing greater improvement in state anxiety and CBT in trait anxiety [59]. These findings emphasize the value of integrated, personalized treatment approaches.

3.2 RQ2: How are Entertainment Computing Technologies Like Virtual Reality (VR), Games, Artificial Intelligence (AI), and Wearable Devices Currently Being Integrated with Specific Biofeedback Interventions for Treating Depression and Anxiety?

Virtual Reality (VR) is increasingly combined with biofeedback to create immersive, interactive environments that enhance engagement and facilitate real-time physiological regulation. Examples include VR systems integrating heart rate variability (HRV) and skin conductance feedback to reduce anxiety [23], respiratory biofeedback visualized via shape-changing artifacts [18], and EEG-based neurofeedback games like *SeekingHeart* for mindfulness training [6]. VR biofeedback has also been applied in exposure therapy, using electrodermal activity (EDA) to monitor anxiety responses [14]. Clinical trials consistently show VR-biofeedback's potential to reduce depressive and anxiety symptoms by providing controlled, multisensory therapeutic experiences [26].

Artificial Intelligence (AI) enhances biofeedback interventions by enabling personalized, adaptive protocols and advanced data analysis. AI-driven EEG analysis has been used in swLORETA Z-score neurofeedback targeting depression [34], while machine learning algorithms predict stress and optimize

HRV biofeedback in healthcare workers [31,41]. AI also facilitates synchronization of multimodal physiological data in VR biofeedback systems [23] and dynamically adjusts virtual environments based on neural markers like frontal alpha asymmetry [22].

Games leverage gamification to increase motivation and adherence, particularly in children and adolescents. EEG neurofeedback games teach self-regulation through engaging interfaces [49,55], while respiratory biofeedback games promote paced breathing to alleviate symptoms [20]. Games often integrate VR and mindfulness elements, combining physiological feedback with immersive, interactive experiences [6].

Wearable devices extend biofeedback beyond clinical settings by enabling continuous physiological monitoring and remote interventions. Devices like the Polar H10 heart rate monitor paired with mobile apps deliver accessible HRV biofeedback [31], while wireless EEG headsets support mobile neurofeedback for depression [27]. Wearables have demonstrated efficacy in diverse populations, including pregnant women and cardiac arrest survivors, enhancing personalization and scalability [13].

3.3   Structured Comparative Framework of Biofeedback Modalities

This section compares the key biofeedback modalities—EEG neurofeedback, HRV biofeedback, VR-based, and gamified biofeedback—across therapeutic efficacy, accessibility, adherence, cost, and technical complexity.

Therapeutic Efficacy. EEG neurofeedback shows strong efficacy in modulating brain activity related to anxiety and depression [32]. HRV biofeedback also demonstrates significant symptom reduction and is supported by multiple RCTs [46]. EDA biofeedback is promising but less studied [23]. VR and gamified biofeedback enhance engagement but face mixed efficacy and personalization challenges [20,30].

Accessibility and Cost. HRV biofeedback is widely accessible and low-cost due to wearable sensors [46]. EEG neurofeedback requires costly equipment and expertise [10]. VR biofeedback has high hardware costs limiting scalability [6]. Gamified biofeedback is generally cost-effective but depends on development complexity [49].

User Adherence and Technical Complexity. HRV biofeedback achieves high adherence with simple use [46]. EEG neurofeedback adherence varies due to session demands [19]. VR biofeedback adherence is limited by cybersickness [30]. Gamified biofeedback improves motivation but requires personalization [20]. Technically, EEG and VR biofeedback are complex, while HRV and gamified systems are more user-friendly.

Overall, HRV biofeedback stands out for its accessibility, low cost, and high adherence, making it a practical option for broad clinical use. EEG neurofeedback offers strong therapeutic efficacy but is limited by higher cost and technical complexity. VR and gamified biofeedback enhance user engagement but face challenges related to usability, personalization, and scalability. These distinctions underscore the importance of tailoring biofeedback modality selection to specific clinical contexts, patient needs, and resource availability.

Note on Evidence Consolidation: Several studies in this review utilize similar intervention platforms, participant populations, or experimental protocols among fMRI neurofeedback (e.g., [19,32,33,37,38]), HRV biofeedback [13,31,41], and VR-based interventions [6,23,26]. To avoid artificial inflation of evidence density, these are interpreted collectively as supporting the efficacy of their respective modalities, rather than as independent validations.

4 Discussion

This systematic review confirms biofeedback as a promising intervention for anxiety and depression, enhanced by technologies such as virtual reality (VR), artificial intelligence (AI), gamification, and wearable devices. These technologies improve patient engagement and enable real-time physiological regulation, although no single biofeedback modality consistently outperforms others, and direct comparative studies remain limited [10,21,58].

Evidence Consolidation and Overlap. Several studies, notably in fMRI neurofeedback and HRV biofeedback, share overlapping samples and methodologies (see Appendix Table 2). To avoid redundancy and inflated evidence density, these findings were synthesized collectively.

Comparative Profiles. fMRI neurofeedback demonstrates strong efficacy but is resource-intensive [32,33,42]. HRV biofeedback is cost-effective with high adherence [13,41,46]. VR and gamified biofeedback enhance user engagement [6,20,30]. Emerging tactile and audio feedback modalities show promise for low-tech, personalized interventions but require further validation [15,28,44].

Usability and Ethical Challenges. Usability challenges remain a significant barrier to clinical scalability. VR biofeedback can induce cybersickness and discomfort, as reported in dental anxiety patients [30]. Wearable devices, such as galvanic skin response units, provide precise monitoring but are vulnerable to motion artifacts and battery limitations, particularly in ambulatory settings [55]. Gamified biofeedback often lacks sufficient personalization, risking symptom trivialization and reduced adherence [20]. Furthermore, interoperability challenges and proprietary restrictions limit seamless integration and customization [17,31]. Ethical considerations around privacy, accessibility, and equity are underexplored. Many interventions require costly hardware, restricting access for marginalized and technology-disadvantaged populations [6]. Privacy risks in biometric data collection are heightened, with few studies implementing robust data protection protocols [23,35]. Most research focuses on short-term outcomes, leaving long-term safety and ethical implications insufficiently addressed [19,29].

Personalization and Population Diversity. Adolescents benefit from combined neurofeedback and cognitive behavioral therapy (CBT) interventions

[58,59], with case studies demonstrating improvements in youth with complex medical and psychological needs. Older adults remain underrepresented, and age-related cognitive and sensory changes necessitate adaptive, simplified interfaces. Technology-disadvantaged groups require low-cost, low-tech alternatives or hybrid clinician-supported models [49]. Notably, therapist-supported remote HRV biofeedback and personalized haptic feedback interventions have demonstrated feasibility and effectiveness in diverse real-world contexts [15,46].

Future Directions. Future research should focus on developing adaptive biofeedback protocols that dynamically adjust feedback complexity and modality based on user age, cognitive capacity, and symptom severity. AI-driven personalization algorithms can optimize treatment by integrating demographic, clinical, and physiological data [43]. The creation of open interoperable platforms that unify multimodal data streams (EEG, HRV, VR) will facilitate comprehensive, real-time feedback and support scalable clinical deployment [17]. Ethical frameworks must prioritize data privacy, equitable access, and long-term monitoring to ensure responsible implementation.

5   Conclusion

This systematic review demonstrates that biofeedback interventions effectively treat depression and anxiety. Advanced technologies like virtual reality (VR), artificial intelligence (AI), and wearable devices have enhanced therapy by improving accessibility, engagement, and convenience. However, significant technical, usability, and ethical challenges—especially concerning data privacy and equitable access—must be addressed. Tailored, user-centered approaches are essential to meet the diverse needs of adolescents, older adults, and technology-disadvantaged groups. While combined psychological and technological treatments show promise, more rigorous comparative and longitudinal studies are needed to confirm long-term benefits and optimize protocols. Future research should develop interoperable platforms, AI-driven personalization, and strong ethical frameworks to ensure privacy and equity. Addressing these challenges will help establish biofeedback as a key tool in mental health care, improving outcomes for those with depression and anxiety.

A   Appendix

Table 2. Summary of Reviewed Biofeedback Studies

Ref	Sample	Mode	Content/Target	Interface	Device/Tech	Main Task/Outcome
[6]	Anxiety, Depression	Visual BF	Real-time physio data	VR game	HTC Vive Pro Eye	Mindfulness with biofeedback in VR
[7]	MDD	RSA BF	HRV, EEG, DMN	Visual	ProComp, EEG	RSA-BF to improve HRV, DMN connect.

continued

Table 2. continued

Ref	Sample	Mode	Content/Target	Interface	Device/Tech	Main Task/Outcome
[13]	Stress, Anxiety, Depression	HRV BF	Paced breathing, HRV	Visual	NeXus-4, Stress Eraser	Daily paced breathing for HRV
[14]	Anxiety	Visual resp. BF	Resp. feedback, SCL, HR	VR	HTC Vive	Breathing regulation in VR for stress reduction
[15]	Anxiety, Stress	Haptic BF	Haptic/thermal patterns	Wrist device	Wearable	Personalized haptic patterns for stress regulation
[16]	Social Anxiety	Video feedback	Icebreaker, trust, LIWC	Video chat	Video chat	Self-disclosure via video chat
[17]	Anxiety	Vibrotactile BF	Vibrotactile stim.	Wrist device	VR device	Just-in-time vibrotactile feedback for stress
[18]	Anxiety, Stress	Haptic BF	Breath sync.	Handheld	Pneumatic device	Breathing exercise with device sync
[20]	Anxiety, Depression, Schiz.	Vis./Aud. BF	EEG complexity, paced breath	Visual/audio	Smartphone/tablet	Paced breathing or game-based balloon BF
[22]	TRD	EEG NF	Alpha/theta modulation	Visual/audio	EEG cap	NF for alpha/theta in depression
[23]	Anxiety	VR BF	HRV, SCL	Visual	VR headset	Compare SCL/HFnu VR-BF for anxiety
[25]	Anxiety	Tactile BF	Wearable affective touch	Wearable	Forearm device	Stroking sensation to mitigate anxiety
[26]	Depression, Anxiety	VR BF	Nature-based relaxation	Visual/audio	Samsung VR, Pro-Comp	VR relaxation with biofeedback
[27]	Anxiety	Audio BF	Music-based neurofeedback	Audio	PC	Listen to transferred music to reduce anxiety
[29]	TRD	FCNef	DLPFC-PCC connectivity	Visual	MRI, Turbo BV	NF to enhance DLPFC-PCC anti-corr.
[30]	Anxiety, Pain	Visual BF	VR distraction, nature	VR	Oculus Quest 2	VR during dental surgery for anxiety/pain
[19]	MDD	fMRI NF	Positive memory recall	NF sessions	MRI, PC	2 sessions, 1-week follow-up
[31]	Anxiety, Cardiac Arrest	HRV BF	Remote HRV, breathing	Visual	App, HR monitor	Daily HRV BF for anxiety
[32]	MDD	fMRI NF	Self-blame bias	Visual	MRI, FRIEND	Self-guided strategies with/without NF
[33]	MDD	fMRI NF	Guilt-specific connect.	Visual	MRI, FRIEND	Modulate ATL-SCC connect. via guilt recall
[34]	MDD, Anxiety	NeuroBF (swLORETA)	Z-score, EEG regions	Visual/audio	Brain Master, Zukor AIR	NF to normalize EEG, reduce symptoms
[35]	Social Anxiety	VR BF	Public speaking, HR/EEG	VR	VR headset	Virtual speech with HR/EEG feedback
[36]	Depression	Vis./Aud. BF	In-game empathy training	VR	Oculus Quest	VR scenarios for empathy
[37]	Anhedonic Depression	fMRI NF	CEN/SN connect.	Visual	MRI, Turbo BV	NF to regulate CEN/SN for symptoms
[38]	Depression	fMRI NF	Insula-dlPFC connect.	Visual	MRI, Turbo BV	NF to modulate emotion regulation
[39]	Anxiety, ASD	HRV BF	HRV training	Visual	emWave, HR monitor	HRV BF for anxiety in ASD
[40]	MDD	NeuroBF	Amygdala activity	Visual	Turbo Brain-Voyager	Recall positive memories for NF

continued

Table 2. continued

Ref	Sample	Mode	Content/Target	Interface	Device/Tech	Main Task/Outcome
[41]	Depression, Stress	HRV BF	HRV, breathing	Visual/audio	ProComp, video	Breathing exercises with feedback
[42]	MDD	fMRI NF	Repetitive negative thinking	Visual	MRI, AFNI	Cognitive reappraisal with NF
[44]	Social Anxiety	Haptic BF	Vibrotactile stimuli	Handheld	Comfort object	Hold vibrotactile prototype during exposure
[46]	Depression	HRV BF	CBT, mindfulness, HRV	Video, msg.	App, HRV sensor	12-week digital CBT with HRV monitoring
[49]	Anxiety	Mobile NeuroBF	Brain state feedback	Visual/audio	Tablet	Relaxation to change brain state, earn tokens
[50]	Social Anxiety	Visual BF	Oxytocin, social learning	Intranasal	fMRI, pupillometry	Oxytocin/placebo with social conditioning
[51]	MDD	fMRI NF	DLPFC up-regulation	Visual	MRI, Turbo BV	Up-regulate DLPFC via BOLD signal
[52]	Depression	fMRI NF	Match healthy brain state	Visual	MRI, Turbo BV	NF guided by brain-state classifier
[54]	Anxiety	SMRNF	SMR, cortisol	Visual/audio	EEG, Bio-Graph	Single session SMR NF for anxiety
[43]	Depression, Rumination	HRV BF	HRV, rumination	Visual	App, ECG belt	At-home HRV BF for rumination
[56]	Anxiety	Videogame NF, CBT	Neurofeedback via game vs. online CBT	Game, text/audio/video (CBT)	PC, internet devices	Anxiety reduction via game-based NF, CBT both reduced anxiety
[57]	Anxiety, Depression	BF+ CBT	BFT: rectal/abdominal EMG, CBT	Visual/verbal (BFT), CBT	Computer (BFT), CBT	Combined BFT+CBT improved anxiety, depression, QoL more than BFT or SoCT alone
[58]	Depression	fMRI NF, CBT	NF: self-regulation of left medial PFC; CBT: ABC model	Visual (NF), CBT	3T MRI, monitor (NF), CBT	Both reduced depression, NF may be integrated into digital health frameworks
[59]	GAD	EEG NF, CBT	NF, CBT	Visual (NF), CBT	EEG system (NF), CBT	Both reduced anxiety, NF better for state anxiety, CBT better for trait anxiety

Abbreviations: BF = Biofeedback; NF = Neurofeedback; fMRI = Functional MRI; TRD = Treatment-resistant depression; SCL = Skin Conductance Level; SMR = Sensorimotor Rhythm; CEN = Central Executive Network; SN = Salience Network; FAA = Frontal Alpha Asymmetry; FCNef = Functional Connectivity Neurofeedback; BOLD = Blood Oxygen Level Dependent; SCP-NF = Slow Cortical Potential Neurofeedback; HEG = Hemoencephalographic Neurofeedback; LORETA = Low-Resolution Electromagnetic Tomography; EMG = Electromyography; DMN = Default Mode Network; DLPFC = Dorsolateral Prefrontal Cortex; PCC = Posterior Cingulate Cortex

References

1. World Health Organization. Anxiety. Fact sheet. https://www.who.int/news-room/fact-sheets/detail/anxiety-disorders. Accessed 19 Feb 2025
2. World Health Organization. Depression. Fact sheet. https://www.who.int/news-room/fact-sheets/detail/depression. Accessed 19 Feb 2025
3. Andersson, G., Titov, N.: Advantages and limitations of Internet-based interventions for common mental disorders. World Psychiatr. **13**(1), 4–11 (2014). https://doi.org/10.1002/wps.20083

4. Lau, C.K.Y., Saad, A., Camara, B., Rahman, D., Bolea-Alamanac, B.: Acceptability of digital mental health interventions for depression and anxiety: systematic review. J. Med. Internet Res. **26**, e52609 (2024). https://doi.org/10.2196/52609

5. Abd-alrazaq, A., et al.: Wearable artificial intelligence for anxiety and depression: scoping review. J. Med. Internet Res. **25**, e42672 (2023). https://doi.org/10.2196/42672

6. Lu, Y., Xue, Y., Ni, S.: SeekingHeart: a biofeedback-based VR game for mindfulness practice. In: Proceedings of the 11th IEEE International Conference on Serious Games and Applications for Health (SeGAH) (2023). https://doi.org/10.1109/SEGAH57547.2023.10253803

7. Patil, A.U., et al.: Review of EEG-based neurofeedback as a therapeutic intervention to treat depression. Psychiatr. Res. Neuroimaging **329**, 111591 (2023). https://doi.org/10.1016/j.pscychresns.2023.111591

8. Alneyadi, M., Drissi, N., Almeqbaali, M., Ouhbi, S.: Biofeedback-based connected mental health interventions for anxiety: systematic literature review. JMIR Mhealth Uhealth **9**(4), e26038 (2021). https://doi.org/10.2196/26038

9. Rommelfanger, K.S., Factor, S.A., LaRoche, S., et al.: Disentangling stigma from functional neurological disorders: conference report and roadmap for the future. Front. Neurol. **8**, 106 (2017). https://doi.org/10.3389/fneur.2017.00106

10. Ratanasiripong, P., Kaewboonchoo, O., Ratanasiripong, N., Hanklang, S., Chumchai, P.: Biofeedback intervention for stress, anxiety, and depression among graduate students in public health nursing. Nutr. Res. Pract. **2015**, 160746 (2015). https://doi.org/10.1155/2015/160746

11. Zotev, V., Mayeli, A., Misaki, M., Bodurka, J.: Emotion self-regulation training in major depressive disorder using simultaneous real-time fMRI and EEG neurofeedback. NeuroImage Clin. **2020**. https://doi.org/10.1016/j.nicl.2020.102331

12. Melnikov, M.Y.: The current evidence levels for biofeedback and neurofeedback interventions in treating depression: a narrative review. Neural Plast. **2021**, 8878857 (2021). https://doi.org/10.1155/2021/8878857

13. van der Zwan, J.E., Huizink, A.C., Lehrer, P.M., Koot, H.M., de Vente, W.: The effect of heart rate variability biofeedback training on mental health of pregnant and non-pregnant women: a randomized controlled trial. Int. J. Environ. Res. Public Health **16**(6) (2019). https://doi.org/10.3390/ijerph16061051. Article 1051

14. Mevlevioğlu, D., Murphy, D., Tabirca, S.: Visual respiratory feedback in virtual reality exposure therapy: a pilot study. In: Proceedings of the 2021 ACM International Conference on Interactive Media Experiences (IMX 2021), Virtual Event, USA, pp. 1–6. Association for Computing Machinery, New York (2021). https://doi.org/10.1145/3452918.3458799

15. Umair, M., Sas, C., Chalabianloo, N., Ersoy, C.: Exploring personalized vibrotactile and thermal patterns for affect regulation. In: Proceedings of the Designing Interactive Systems Conference 2021 (DIS 2021). ACM, New York (2021). https://doi.org/10.1145/3461778.3462042

16. Miller, M.K., Dechant, M.J., Mandryk, R.L.: Meeting you, seeing me: the role of social anxiety, visual feedback, and interface layout in a get-to-know-you task via video chat. In: Proceedings of the 2021 CHI Conference on Human Factors in Computing Systems (CHI 2021), Yokohama, Japan, Article 339, 14 pages. Association for Computing Machinery, New York (2021). https://doi.org/10.1145/3411764.3445664

17. Raether, J., Haque, E., Chaspari, T.: Evaluating just-in-time vibrotactile feedback for communication anxiety. In: Proceedings of the International Conference on

Multimodal Interaction (ICMI 2022), p. 11. ACM, New York (2022). https://doi.org/10.1145/3536221.3556590

18. Farrall, A., Taylor, J., Ainsworth, B., Alexander, J.: Manifesting breath: empirical evidence for the integration of shape-changing biofeedback-based artefacts within digital mental health interventions. In: Proceedings of the 2023 CHI Conference on Human Factors in Computing Systems (CHI 2023), Hamburg, Germany, p. 14. ACM (2023). https://doi.org/10.1145/3544548.3581188

19. Compère, L., Siegle, G.J., Riley, E., Lazzaro, S., et al.: Enhanced efficacy of CBT following augmentation with amygdala rtfMRI neurofeedback in depression. J. Affect. Disord. **339**, 495–501 (2023). https://doi.org/10.1016/j.jad.2023.07.063

20. Khan, M., Hadjileontiadis, L., Cornforth, D.J., Drummond, J., Jelinek, H.F.: The effectiveness of point-of-care testing with intervention in psychopathology: a pilot study. In: Proceedings of the 2021 14th International Congress on Image and Signal Processing, BioMedical Engineering and Informatics (CISP-BMEI). IEEE (2021). https://doi.org/10.1109/CISP-BMEI53629.2021.9624223

21. Banerjee, S., Argáez, C.: Neurofeedback and Biofeedback for Mood and Anxiety Disorders: A Review of Clinical Effectiveness and Guidelines. Canadian Agency for Drugs and Technologies in Health, Ottawa (2017). https://www.ncbi.nlm.nih.gov/books/NBK531603/

22. Wang, S.M., et al.: Rapid onset of intranasal esketamine in patients with treatment resistant depression and major depression with suicide ideation: a meta-analysis. Clin. Psychopharmacol. Neurosci. **19**(2), 341–354 (2021). https://doi.org/10.9758/cpn.2021.19.2.341

23. Baldini, A., Patron, E., Gentili, C., Scilingo, E.P., Greco, A.: Novel VR-based biofeedback systems: a comparison between heart rate variability- and electrodermal activity-driven approaches. IEEE Trans. Affective Comput. (2024). https://doi.org/10.1109/TAFFC.2024.3352424

24. Park, S.M., Jung, H.Y.: Respiratory sinus arrhythmia biofeedback alters heart rate variability and default mode network connectivity in major depressive disorder: a preliminary study. Int. J. Psychophysiol. **158**, 225–237 (2020). https://doi.org/10.1016/j.ijpsycho.2020.10.008

25. Zhao, Y., Tao, Y., Le, G., Maki, R., et al.: Affective touch as immediate and passive wearable intervention. Proc. ACM Interact. Mob. Wearable Ubiquitous Technol. **6**(4) (2023). https://doi.org/10.1109/IMWUT57547.2023.10253803. Article 200

26. Cho, Y., et al.: Effect of virtual reality-based biofeedback for depressive and anxiety symptoms: randomized controlled study. J. Affect. Disord. **361**, 392–398 (2024). https://doi.org/10.1016/j.jad.2024.06.031

27. Hou, Y., Zhang, S., Li, N., Huang, Z., et al.: Neurofeedback training improves anxiety trait and depressive symptom in GAD. Brain Behav. **11**(2), e02024 (2021). https://doi.org/10.1002/brb3.2024

28. Hu, Z., Liu, Y., Chen, G., Zhong, S., Zhang, A.: Make your favorite music curative: music style transfer for anxiety reduction. In: Proceedings of the 28th ACM International Conference on Multimedia (MM 2020), pp. 1–5. ACM, Seattle (2020). https://doi.org/10.1145/3394171.3414070

29. Takamura, M., et al.: Antidepressive effect of left dorsolateral prefrontal cortex neurofeedback in patients with major depressive disorder: a preliminary report. J. Affect. Disord. **271**, 224–227 (2020). https://doi.org/10.1016/j.jad.2020.03.080

30. Ghobadi, A., Moradpoor, H., Sharini, H., Khazaie, H., Moradpoor, P.: The effect of virtual reality on reducing patients' anxiety and pain during dental implant surgery. BMC Oral Health **24**, 186 (2024). https://doi.org/10.1186/s12903-024-03904-8

31. Birk, J.L., Cumella, R., Lopez-Veneros, D., Agarwal, S., Kronish, I.M.: Feasibility of a remote heart rate variability biofeedback intervention for reducing anxiety in cardiac arrest survivors: a pilot trial. Contemp. Clin. Trials. Commun. **37**, 101251 (2024). https://doi.org/10.1016/j.conctc.2023.101251

32. Jaeckle, T., Williams, S.C.R., Barker, G.J., Basilio, R., et al.: Self-blame in major depression: a randomised pilot trial comparing fMRI neurofeedback with self-guided psychological strategies. Psychol. Med. **53**(7), 2831–2841 (2023). https://doi.org/10.1017/S0033291721004797. Cambridge University Press

33. Zahn, R., Moll, J., Paiva, M., Garrido, G., et al.: Blame-rebalance fMRI neurofeedback in major depressive disorder: a randomised proof-of-concept trial. NeuroImage Clin. **24**, 101992 (2019). https://doi.org/10.1016/j.nicl.2019.101992

34. Wu, Y.-C., Yu, H.-E., Yen, C.-F., Yeh, Y.-C., et al.: The effects of swLORETA Z-score neurofeedback for patients comorbid with major depressive disorder and anxiety symptoms. J. Affect. Disord. **350**, 340–349 (2024). https://doi.org/10.1016/j.jad.2024.01.020

35. Premkumar, P.: Corrigendum: augmenting self-guided virtual-reality exposure therapy for social anxiety with biofeedback: a randomised controlled trial. Front. Psychiatry **16**, 1548762 (2025). https://doi.org/10.3389/fpsyt.2025.1548762

36. Li, Y., Huang, A., Sanku, B., He, J.: Designing an empathy training for depression prevention using virtual reality and a preliminary study. In: Proceedings of the 2023 IEEE Conference on Virtual Reality 3D User Interfaces Abstracts Workshops (VRW) (2023). https://doi.org/10.1109/VRW57547.2023.10253803

37. Wang, X., Zhou, X., Li, J., et al.: A feasibility study of goal-directed network-based real-time fMRI neurofeedback for anhedonic depression. *Front. Psychiatry* **14**, 1253727 (2023). https://doi.org/10.3389/fpsyt.2023.1253727

38. Maywald, M., Paolini, M., Rauchmann, B.S., et al.: Individual- and connectivity-based real-time fMRI neurofeedback to modulate emotion-related brain responses in patients with depression: a pilot study. Brain Sci. **12**(12), 1714 (2022). https://doi.org/10.3390/brainsci12121714

39. Coleman, R., Trites, K., Parker, B., Benson, N.: Heart rate variability biofeedback as an anxiety intervention for college students with autism spectrum disorder. Rese. Autism Spectr. Disord. **110**, 102300 (2024). https://doi.org/10.1016/j.rasd.2023.102300

40. Compère, L., Siegle, G.J., Young, K.: Importance of test-retest reliability for promoting fMRI based screening and interventions in major depressive disorder. Transl. Psychiatry **11**, 387 (2021). https://doi.org/10.1038/s41398-021-01507-3

41. Hsieh, H.-F., Huang, I.-C., Liu, Y., Chen, W.-L., Lee, Y.-W., Hsu, H.-T.: The effects of biofeedback training and smartphone-delivered biofeedback training on resilience, occupational stress, and depressive symptoms among abused psychiatric nurses. Int. J. Environ. Res. Public Health **17**(8), 2905 (2020). https://doi.org/10.3390/ijerph17082905

42. Tsuchiyagaito, A., et al.: Real-time fMRI functional connectivity neurofeedback reducing repetitive negative thinking in depression: a double-blind, randomized. Sham-Controlled Proof-of-Concept Trial. Psychother. Psychosom. **92**(2), 87–100 (2023). https://doi.org/10.1159/000528377

43. Schumann, A., Helbing, N., Rieger, K., Suttkus, S., Bär, K.-J.: Depressive rumination and heart rate variability: a pilot study on the effect of biofeedback on rumination and its physiological concomitants. Front. Psychiatry **13**, 961294 (2022). https://doi.org/10.3389/fpsyt.2022.961294

44. Macdonald, S., Freeman, E., Pollick, F., Brewster, S.: Prototyping and evaluation of emotionally resonant vibrotactile comfort objects as a calming social anxiety intervention. ACM Trans. Comput.-Hum. Interact. (2024). https://doi.org/10.1145/3648615

45. Bloom, P.A., Pagliaccio, D., Zhang, J., Bauer, C.C., et al.: Mindfulness-based real-time fMRI neurofeedback: a randomized controlled trial to optimize dosing for depressed adolescents. BMC Psychiatry **23**, 757 (2023). https://doi.org/10.1186/s12888-023-05223-8

46. Forman-Hoffman, V.L., Sihvonen, S., Wielgosz, J., Kuhnc, E., Nelson, B.W., et al.: Therapist-supported digital mental health intervention for depressive symptoms: a randomized clinical trial. J. Affect. Disord. **349**, 494–501 (2024). https://doi.org/10.1016/j.jad.2024.01.057

47. Fernández-Alvarez, J., González-Rodríguez, A., Pérez-García, M., Molinero, A.: Biofeedback in the treatment of depression and anxiety: a comprehensive review. J. Clin. Psychol. **78**(4), 567–589 (2022). https://doi.org/10.1002/jclp.23211

48. Whiston, A., et al.: Examining stress and residual symptoms in remitted and partially remitted depression using a wearable electrodermal activity device: a pilot study. IEEE J. Transl. Eng. Health Med. **11** (2022). https://doi.org/10.1109/JTEHM.2022.3228483. Art. no. 3228483

49. Antle, A.N., McLaren, E.-S., Fiedler, H., Johnson, N.: Evaluating the impact of a mobile neurofeedback app for young children at school and home. In: Proceedings of the 2019 CHI Conference on Human Factors in Computing Systems (CHI 2019), pp. 1–13. ACM, New York (2019). https://doi.org/10.1145/3290605.3300266

50. Flechsenhar, A., Levine, S.M., Müller, L.E., Herpertz, S.C., Bertsch, K.: Oxytocin and social learning in socially anxious men and women. Neuropharmacology **251**, 109930 (2024). https://doi.org/10.1016/j.neuropharm.2024.109930

51. Takamura, M., et al.: Application of functional connectivity neurofeedback in patients with treatment-resistant depression: a preliminary report. J. Affect. Disord. Rep. **14**, 100644 (2023). https://doi.org/10.1016/j.jadr.2023.100644

52. Pereira, J.A., et al.: A real-time fMRI neurofeedback system for the clinical alleviation of depression with a subject-independent classification of brain states: a proof of principle study. Front. Hum. Neurosci. **16**, 933559 (2022). https://doi.org/10.3389/fnhum.2022.933559

53. Robinson, T., Condell, J., Ramsey, E., Leavey, G.: Self-management of subclinical common mental health disorders (anxiety, depression and sleep disorders) using wearable devices. Int. J. Environ. Res. Public Health **20**(3), 2636 (2023). https://doi.org/10.3390/ijerph20032636

54. Gadea, M., Aliño, M., Hidalgo, V., Espert, R., Salvador, A.: Effects of a single session of SMR neurofeedback training on anxiety and cortisol levels. Clin. Neurophysiol. **50**(3), 167–173 (2020). https://doi.org/10.1016/j.neucli.2020.03.001

55. Yu, M., Bai, Y., Li, Y.: Emo-regulator: an emotion-regulation training system fusing virtual reality and EEG-based neurofeedback. In: Proceedings of the 45th Annual International Conference of the IEEE Engineering in Medicine Biology Society (EMBC), pp. 1–4 (2023). https://doi.org/10.1109/EMBC40787.2023.10340975

56. Tsui, T.Y.L., DeFrance, K., Khalid-Khan, S., Granic, I., Hollenstein, T.: Reductions of anxiety symptoms, state anxiety, and anxious arousal in youth playing the videogame mindlight compared to online cognitive behavioral therapy. Games Health J. **10**(5), 330–338 (2021). https://doi.org/10.1089/g4h.2020.0083

57. Nikjooy, A., Khoshlahjeh Sedgh, A., Mahjoubi, B., Mirzaei, R., Naziri, M., Mirbehresi, P.: The effects of cognitive behavioral therapy with biofeedback therapy on the quality of life, anxiety, depression and somatic symptoms in patients with dyssynergic defecation: a randomized controlled trial. Med. J. Islam. Repub. Iran **36**, 74 (2022). https://doi.org/10.47176/mjiri.36.74

58. Mel'nikov, M.Y.: Real-time fMRI neurofeedback compared to cognitive behavioral therapy in a pilot study for the treatment of mild and moderate depression. Eur. Arch. Psychiatry Clin. Neurosci. **273**(5), 1139–1149 (2023). https://doi.org/10.1007/s00406-022-01462-0

59. Salama, A., Abdel-Latif, S., Omar, T., El Wafa, H.A.: Neurofeedback training and cognitive behavior therapy for treatment of generalized anxiety disorder in children and adolescents: a comparative study. NeuroRegulation **9**(1), 29–38 (2022). https://doi.org/10.15540/NR.9.1.29

Chatbots in Children's Collaborative Making: Exploring Challenges and Implications for Interaction Design

Xinqi Feng[2], Lei Cai[1], Weiwei Liu[1], and Xusheng Zhang[1(✉)]

[1] College of Comupter Science and Technology, Zhejiang University, Hangzhou, China
zhangxs001@zju.edu.cn
[2] Polytechnic Institute, Zhejiang University, Hangzhou, China

Abstract. With the increasing integration of chatbots into educational settings, their role in supporting children's collaborative creativity remains underexplored. This study investigates how children aged 9–12 interact with a chatbot during a real-world maker task and what challenges emerge in the process. Using a qualitative approach, we conducted four workshop-based group activities in a primary school setting, where children used the Grove Zero platform and the Doubao chatbot to collaboratively design prototypes for real-life problems. Data were collected through field observations and semi-structured interviews and analyzed using thematic analysis. The findings reveal three key challenges: (1) breakdowns in communication caused by children's vague expressions; (2) disrupted collaboration due to changes in group roles and reduced peer interaction; and (3) growing behavioral dependence on chatbot over time. Based on these insights, we propose three design strategies: guided language scaffolding, collaboration-aware interaction design, and heuristic-based chatbot responses. This study offers practical implications for the development of child-centered educational AI systems.

Keywords: Chatbot · Collaborative Making · Child–AI Interaction

1 Introduction

With the advancement of artificial intelligence, chatbots have become increasingly present in children's learning and creative activities as intelligent companions. Centered on natural language interaction, they simulate human dialogue to provide immediate feedback and cognitive support [13]. For children aged 9 to 12, chatbots help reduce technical barriers and promote engagement in exploration, communication, and collaboration [12]. At the same time, maker education—emphasizing hands-on, interdisciplinary, and collaborative learning—has gained traction in primary education. Maker tasks foster both technical problem-solving and higher-order social cognition through iterative teamwork [15]. However, younger learners often face challenges such as cognitive overload and unbalanced

© IFIP International Federation for Information Processing 2025
Published by Springer Nature Switzerland AG 2025
R. Yamanishi et al. (Eds.): ICEC 2025 Workshops, LNCS 15935, pp. 52–60, 2025.
https://doi.org/10.1007/978-3-032-02534-0_7

collaboration [3]. In this context, chatbots offer new potential to support children's maker participation by facilitating ideation, problem-solving, and coordination [24]. Yet, most existing studies focus on individual learning, with little attention to chatbots' roles, limitations, and design needs in collaborative creation [25,26]. This study explores how children aged 9–12 interact with chatbots during collaborative making. Using workshop observations and interviews, we identify usage patterns, challenges, and derive design strategies to inform future development of child-centered AI interaction systems.

2   Related Work

2.1   The Role of Chatbots in Supporting Children's Learning

Conversational AI, which enables interaction through natural language, has increasingly been used to support children's learning. Typical forms include voice assistants, chatbots, and virtual companions, often designed with anthropomorphic or emotionally expressive features to enhance engagement and reduce technical barriers [7,13]. Prior studies have shown that such systems can promote positive learning behaviors, including greater verbal output, more frequent questioning, and increased task involvement [5,21]. Chatbots have also been applied across domains like language learning and science education, offering real-time feedback and personalized prompts that facilitate adaptive and differentiated learning [9,24–26].

However, challenges remain. Children may struggle to formulate clear queries, and most chatbots are designed for individual use, offering limited support for peer collaboration [6,12,22]. In group settings, AI responses may not align with shared goals or support joint meaning-making. This calls for systems that better account for the social and communicative dynamics of collaborative learning.

Recent work highlights the potential of generative AI to fill this gap. For example, Wei et al. found that tools like ChatGPT enhanced team creativity and content co-construction in digital storytelling, though risks of over-reliance remain [23]. Nguyen et al. further showed that embodied AI in mixed reality settings supported self- and co-regulated learning [16]. These findings point to a shift in AI's role—from content delivery to facilitating collaboration.

Yet, research remains limited in unstructured, hands-on contexts like maker education, where real-time coordination and peer interaction are central. This raises new design questions for supporting collaborative learning through conversational AI in open-ended settings.

2.2   Collaborative Making in Children's Maker Education

Maker education, which integrates science, technology, engineering, arts, and mathematics, emphasizes hands-on practice, creative thinking, and interdisciplinary problem-solving. In children's learning contexts, it promotes not only active participation but also collaborative making as a key process for social learning and collective knowledge construction.

Collaborative making involves multiple learners jointly designing, building, or solving problems through shared goals, distributed tasks, and iterative feedback. These activities cultivate children's communication, negotiation, and teamwork skills while engaging them in authentic, cognitively demanding scenarios [11,17]. Studies have shown that such environments enhance conceptual understanding, engagement, and creative outcomes [14,17]. For instance, Vongkulluksn et al. found that children achieved cognitive transfer through sharing and social construction [18], while Bers highlighted collaboration itself as a powerful learning experience when using programming toys and electronic kits [2].

Nonetheless, challenges such as conflict, miscommunication, and unequal participation are common, especially in complex tasks [8]. To address this, strategies like scaffolding, role assignment, and technological mediation have been proposed to optimize collaborative quality [20]. In sum, collaborative making plays a vital role in maker education. Investigating its interactional dynamics and challenges lays the groundwork for designing effective support systems, including chatbot-based interventions.

3   Research Methods

This study adopts an exploratory, inductive approach to examine how chatbots support children aged 9–12 in collaborative making. It focuses on identifying challenges encountered during hands-on creative tasks involving chatbot interaction. Data were collected through semi-structured interviews and structured observations, and analyzed using thematic analysis.

3.1   Research Setting

This study was conducted within a collaborative maker task involving children aged 9 to 12, using Grove Zero for modular hardware assembly and Codecraft for block-based programming. Children worked in small groups to identify real-world problems and build functional prototypes through a three-phase process: ideation, assembly, and programming.

To support the task, we developed a custom chatbot agent based on Doubao, a Chinese-language conversational system. The agent retained basic natural language capabilities and was adapted to the maker context, offering lightweight assistance through open-ended dialogue. It was embedded across all task stages: stimulating idea generation during ideation, providing technical help during assembly, and offering logic guidance during programming. While not designed for deep context tracking, the agent functioned as an embedded support tool, enabling us to observe how children used conversational AI in real-time collaboration and how its affordances and limitations shaped group interaction.

3.2   Participants

Twelve children (aged 9–12; 6 girls, 6 boys) were recruited from a primary school with maker education experience. All participants had basic familiarity with

Scratch or Codecraft. None had used Doubao prior to the study. As shown in Table 1, a brief standardized introduction was provided to ensure consistent understanding before the task. Observed interaction behaviors were interpreted as emerging from in-task dynamics.

Table 1. Demographic information for twelve children participating in the workshop.

ID	Gender	Age	AI Exp.	Doubao Exp.	Maker Exp. (Years)	Group
P1	Female	9	No	No	0.5	A
P2	Male	10	Yes	No	1	A
P3	Female	10	No	No	1	A
P4	Male	11	Yes	No	1	B
P5	Male	11	No	No	0.5	B
P6	Female	12	Yes	No	2	B
P7	Female	10	No	No	1	C
P8	Male	12	Yes	No	2	C
P9	Male	11	Yes	No	1	C
P10	Female	9	No	No	0.5	D
P11	Male	10	No	No	1	D
P12	Female	12	Yes	No	1.5	D

3.3   Data Collection

The research team conducted real-time observations to document when and how children interacted with Doubao, including initiation, frequency, and behavioral responses to feedback. After the task, each group participated in individual interviews, which were audio-recorded and transcribed to capture their experiences with the chatbot.

3.4   Data Analysis

All interview recordings were transcribed and analyzed using thematic analysis in NVivo, following the guidelines of Braun and Clarke [4]. A preliminary coding framework was developed based on the interview protocol and initial data review. Open coding was then conducted, with codes iteratively revised and refined. This process initially yielded six themes and fifteen sub-themes. After further review, the final structure was streamlined to six sub-themes organized under three overarching themes.

4 Reults

4.1 Breakdowns in Communication

Task Contextualization. Some children exhibited unclear or incomplete contextual expression when making requests to the AI, which led to misunderstandings and irrelevant responses. In one task, a child asked Doubao, "We're making a water reminder—how do we do it?" The AI responded with a generic solution, prompting the child to clarify, "That's not what I meant—I want to know how it makes a sound." This interaction illustrates a misinterpretation of the vague phrase "how to do it," in which the AI failed to address the core objective. The incident highlights how children often use conversational rather than task-specific language, lacking structured articulation of their problem. In another group, a child asked during the assembly phase, "How do I make the light blink?" Without specifying the hardware module or programming platform, the AI defaulted to providing a pseudocode-like explanation rather than offering guidance tailored to Codecraft.

Spatial Language. During the hands-on construction process, we observed that children commonly relied on vague deictic expressions—such as "this," "that," or "here"—to describe spatial relationships between modules and components, rather than using precise names or logical references. For example, while operating onsite, P9 attempted to seek help from Doubao by asking, "Why isn't it lighting up? Did I connect this part wrong?" The chatbot responded with a standard power-checking procedure. However, due to the ambiguous use of "it" and "this part," the suggestion failed to resolve the actual issue. In a follow-up interview, P9 recalled, "When I said 'it isn't lighting up,' I actually meant the light on the left."

A similar issue occurred in P11's group. While debugging, P11 asked, "If I connect this wire here, will it light up?" The chatbot suggested verifying the port number, but in fact, P11 had connected the wire to an uninitialized output port. Since the child did not specify what "here" referred to, the chatbot was unable to accurately identify the source of the problem (Table 2).

Table 2. Themes and Subthemes generated during the thematic analysis process.

Theme	Subthemes
Breakdowns in Communication	Task Context Spatial Language
Modes of Collaboration	Role Shifts Social Interaction
From Exploration to Dependence	Real-Time Assistance Creative Output

4.2   Modes of Collaboration

Role Shifts. Observations revealed that in most groups, children spontaneously established clear task roles at the beginning of the activity. For example, in Group B, P4 was responsible for information retrieval, P5 handled the physical construction, and P6 took charge of programming. However, once Doubao was introduced into the workflow, these established role boundaries began to blur. Some children frequently crossed their designated responsibilities to interact directly with the AI, leading to moments of coordination breakdown within the group. This pattern of role disruption was observed repeatedly across multiple groups.

Social Interaction. During AI-assisted sessions, shifts in group interaction patterns were observed, particularly in how individual children engaged with peers versus the chatbot. In several cases, children who initially participated actively in group dialogue began directing their questions primarily to the AI, reducing verbal exchange with teammates.

In the construction phase of Group C, for example, participant P8 encountered difficulty connecting the power module—a moment that could have prompted peer discussion. Instead, P8 asked the chatbot, "How do I connect the power cable?" and, after receiving a response, completed the task independently. Observation notes recorded: "Following the connection, P7 resumed building silently, while P7 and P9 continued working separately. No verbal coordination occurred for over four minutes." Interview data supported this pattern. P9 remarked, "He just kept asking the AI. Later we didn't really solve things together." P8 added, "I didn't understand what the AI was saying, so I just stopped following."

4.3   Cognitive Dependence

Real-Time Assistance. Across most groups, we observed a notable behavioral shift: once children realized that the AI could provide relatively clear answers or actionable suggestions, they began to treat it as their primary source of information, gradually abandoning their original exploratory approaches. For example, during the initial ideation phase in Group A, P1 hesitated over whether to use a voice module. After an inconclusive discussion with teammates, P1 asked Doubao, "Can this module record sound?" The AI responded accurately, explaining both the module's function and wiring instructions. From that point onward, P1 began to consult the AI frequently to confirm each step of the design. During the construction phase, P1 even posed preemptive questions before encountering any real issues, such as, "Is it okay if we connect it like this?" Observation notes indicated that team members in this group rarely engaged in self-verification or peer discussion during subsequent stages. Instead, they consistently relied on the AI as a "decision validator." P4 echoed this tendency in the interview: "At first, I asked it just for fun. But then I realized it was usually right, so I just followed what it said."

Convergence of Ideas. Another manifestation of cognitive dependence emerged in the realm of creative output. Although the AI was intended to serve as a heuristic tool—to stimulate divergent thinking and expand children's imagination—in some groups, its suggestions were directly "copied and executed," resulting in idea convergence and diminished originality. When tasked with designing a solution for "how to remind someone to water the plants," the group initially proposed several creative directions, such as using wind chimes or setting up a countdown light. However, after P12 asked Doubao, "What are some creative ways to remind people to water the plants?", the AI provided three typical solutions, including a humidity sensor linked to a buzzer. The group quickly abandoned their original ideas and adopted the AI's suggestion instead, repeatedly emphasizing during the build phase that "this is the one the AI said is better." In the interview, P11 admitted, "I felt like what it said was already the best solution."

5   Discussion

The findings of this study reveal critical design challenges when integrating chatbots into children's collaborative making tasks. Based on observed interaction breakdowns, role imbalances, and behavioral dependence, we propose three key directions for improving chatbot design in educational settings: adaptive language scaffolding, social awareness, and heuristic feedback.

5.1   Design Implications

First, mismatches between children's expressive abilities and chatbot responses often disrupted interaction flow and comprehension. From a sociocultural perspective, effective learning occurs within the zone of proximal development (ZPD), where assistance should be appropriately scaffolded [22]. To better align with children's developmental levels, chatbot systems should offer adaptive language support—such as simplified or segmented feedback, adjustable response lengths, and pacing options. Prior work has shown that child-agent interactions are more effective when linguistic complexity matches children's cognitive readiness [12].

Second, the chatbot's inability to recognize group dynamics sometimes led to uneven participation, where one child dominated the AI interaction while others withdrew. These patterns echo earlier findings that AI systems lacking social awareness can unintentionally disrupt peer collaboration [19]. To promote balanced group engagement, chatbot systems could include social coordination features—such as tracking turn-taking, prompting quieter members, or inviting team-based decisions—to preserve equitable collaboration and reinforce shared regulation processes [10].

Finally, repeated reliance on chatbot-generated solutions led to cognitive dependence, where children bypassed peer discussion or self-reflection. From a sociocultural standpoint, this undermines learning by disrupting the process of internalization through guided interaction. Belpaeme et al. report similar tendencies in child-robot studies, where AI systems perceived as authoritative reduce learner autonomy [1]. To mitigate this, chatbot feedback should adopt a heuristic, inquiry-based approach, encouraging children to consider alternatives, reflect, and involve teammates—thereby reinforcing their agency and keeping them within the ZPD as active co-constructors of knowledge.

5.2   Limitations and Future Research

While this study offers initial insights into children's collaboration with conversational AI, it has limitations. The small sample limits generalizability, suggesting future research should span more diverse maker tasks. Additionally, the short-term workshop setting restricted observations of long-term AI use. Longitudinal studies are needed to explore how children's interactions with AI evolve over time in sustained collaborative learning.

6   Conclusion

This study explored how children aged 9–12 engage in collaborative maker tasks with a chatbot, using field observation and semi-structured interviews. We identified three themes that illuminate the dual role of chatbots as helpful partners and as potential disruptors fostering cognitive dependence. From these insights, we offer three design implications: (1) tailor question-and-answer prompts to children's expressive styles; (2) embed social-awareness features to ensure balanced collaboration; and (3) use heuristic, open-ended feedback to sustain inquiry and creativity. These guidelines provide practical direction for designing AI tools that support effective, child-centered learning in maker environments.

References

1. Belpaeme, T., Kennedy, J., Ramachandran, A., Scassellati, B., Tanaka, F.: Social robots for education: a review. Sci. Robot. **3**(21), eaat5954 (2018)
2. Bers, M.U.: Coding as a Playground: Programming and Computational Thinking in the Early Childhood Classroom. Routledge (2020)
3. Blikstein, P.: Maker movement in education: history and prospects. In: de Vries, M. (ed.) Handbook of Technology Education, pp. 419–437. Springer, Cham (2018). https://doi.org/10.1007/978-3-319-44687-5_33
4. Braun, V., Clarke, V.: Using thematic analysis in psychology. Qual. Res. Psychol. **3**(2), 77–101 (2006)
5. Breazeal, C., Dautenhahn, K., Kanda, T.: Social robotics. In: Siciliano, B., Khatib, O. (eds.) Springer Handbook of Robotics, pp. 1935–1972. Springer, Cham (2016). https://doi.org/10.1007/978-3-319-32552-1_72
6. Bruner, J.S.: Toward a Theory of Instruction. Harvard University Press (1974)
7. Caruana, N., Moffat, R., Miguel-Blanco, A., Cross, E.S.: Perceptions of intelligence & sentience shape children's interactions with robot reading companions. Sci. Rep. **13**(1), 7341 (2023)

8. Chan, C.K., van Aalst, J.: Knowledge building: theory, design, and analysis. In: International Handbook of the Learning Sciences, pp. 295–307. Routledge (2018)

9. Fryer, L., Carpenter, R.: Bots as language learning tools (2006)

10. Hadwin, A.F., Järvelä, S., Miller, M.: Self-regulated, co-regulated, and socially shared regulation of learning. In: Handbook of Self-regulation of Learning and Performance, vol. 30, pp. 65–84 (2011)

11. Halverson, E.R., Sheridan, K.: The maker movement in education. Harv. Educ. Rev. **84**(4), 495–504 (2014)

12. Kory-Westlund, J.M., Breazeal, C.: A long-term study of young children's rapport, social emulation, and language learning with a peer-like robot playmate in preschool. Front. Robot. AI **6**, 81 (2019)

13. Kuhail, M.A., Alturki, N., Alramlawi, S., Alhejori, K.: Interacting with educational chatbots: a systematic review. Educ. Inf. Technol. **28**(1), 973–1018 (2023)

14. Lee, D.C., Chang, C.Y.: Evaluating self-directed learning competencies in digital learning environments: a meta-analysis. Educ. Inf. Technol. **30**, 1–22 (2024)

15. Martin, L.: The promise of the maker movement for education. J. Pre-College Eng. Educ. Res. (J-PEER) **5**(1), 4 (2015)

16. Nguyen, A., Gul, F., Dang, B., Huynh, L., Tuunanen, T.: Designing embodied generative artificial intelligence in mixed reality for active learning in higher education. Innov. Educ. Teach. Int., 1–16 (2025)

17. Resnick, M., et al.: Scratch: programming for all. Commun. ACM **52**(11), 60–67 (2009)

18. Santos, E.M.F., da Silva, C.G., de Deus Lopes, R.: School Maker Environments: A Systematic Review of Makerspaces in k-12 Education. Heliyon (2024)

19. Serholt, S., et al.: The case of classroom robots: teachers' deliberations on the ethical tensions. AI Soc. **32**, 613–631 (2017)

20. Shak, M.: The emergence of leadership in pre-service teacher education students' collaborative learning in the context of maker education project. Master's thesis, M. Shak (2023)

21. Tanaka, F., Matsuzoe, S.: Children teach a care-receiving robot to promote their learning: field experiments in a classroom for vocabulary learning. J. Hum.-Robot Interact. **1**(1), 78–95 (2012)

22. Vygotsky, L.S.: Mind in Society: The Development of Higher Psychological Processes, vol. 86. Harvard University Press (1978)

23. Wei, X., Wang, L., Lee, L.K., Liu, R.: The effects of generative AI on collaborative problem-solving and team creativity performance in digital story creation: an experimental study. Int. J. Educ. Technol. High. Educ. **22**(1), 23 (2025)

24. Winkler, R., Söllner, M.: Unleashing the potential of chatbots in education: a state-of-the-art analysis. In: Academy of Management Proceedings, vol. 2018, p. 15903. Academy of Management Briarcliff Manor (2018)

25. Wollny, S., Schneider, J., Di Mitri, D., Weidlich, J., Rittberger, M., Drachsler, H.: Are we there yet?-a systematic literature review on chatbots in education. Front. Artif. Intell. **4**, 654924 (2021)

26. Zawacki-Richter, O., Marín, V.I., Bond, M., Gouverneur, F.: Systematic review of research on artificial intelligence applications in higher education-where are the educators? Int. J. Educ. Technol. High. Educ. **16**(1), 1–27 (2019)

Exploring Psychologist Applied Biomarkers in Bipolar Disorder: A Systematic Framework

Minhazul Islam[ID], Mengru Xue$^{(\boxtimes)}$[ID], and Tasnim Afra[ID]

Ningbo Global Innovation Center, Zhejiang University, Ningbo, China
mengruxue@zju.edu.cn

Abstract. Bipolar disorder (BD) is a multifaceted mental illness characterised by alternating manic or hypomanic and depressed episodes. The present diagnosis is predominantly based on subjective assessments, frequently resulting in delays and misdiagnosis because of symptom overlap with other conditions. Notwithstanding progress in biomarker research, their incorporation into clinical practice is still constrained, underscoring a significant deficiency in objective diagnostic instruments for BD. This study examined qualitative interviews with seven mental health professionals to determine essential biomarker criteria and propose enhancements for bipolar disorder diagnosis. Research indicates constraints in subjective diagnosis methods and underscores the promise of integrating digital tools with biomarkers to improve precision. Essential characteristics for data-driven decision-making were identified to facilitate early detection and action. The study advocates for user-friendly digital health tools for clinicians that incorporate biomarkers to enhance the diagnosis and management of bipolar disorder. These insights facilitate the development of a paradigm aimed at improving long-term patient outcomes.

Keywords: Bipolar disorder · Biomarkers · Digital health tools · Diagnostic accuracy · Early diagnosis · Patient engagement

1 Introduction

BD is characterized by alternating episodes of mania or hypomania and depression, severely impairing daily functioning [31]. It impacts almost 50 million individuals worldwide and is linked to considerable morbidity and death, including elevated risks of suicide and comorbidities such as diabetes and cardiovascular illnesses [25,27]. Contemporary diagnostic techniques, based on DSM-5 and ICD criteria, are constrained by the absence of objective biomarkers, resulting in diagnostic delays and mistakes [13].

The present diagnosis of BD predominantly depends on subjective evaluations, potentially resulting in biases and delays [10,16]. Despite the potential of biomarker research, its incorporation into clinical practice is constrained due to the absence of objective methods for precise and early diagnosis [1,18,22,37].

© IFIP International Federation for Information Processing 2025
Published by Springer Nature Switzerland AG 2025
R. Yamanishi et al. (Eds.): ICEC 2025 Workshops, LNCS 15935, pp. 61–75, 2025.
https://doi.org/10.1007/978-3-032-02534-0_8

This gap obstructs prompt business development identification. Existing techniques are hampered by the paucity of objective biomarkers and holistic diagnostic frameworks [3,14,29]. This study analyses physicians' views on using biological and behavioural biomarkers in diagnostic instruments to better early bipolar illness diagnosis and treatment, developing a more objective diagnostic framework. A qualitative review of mental health experts' data suggests design changes to increase diagnostic accuracy [2].

This research involved semi-structured interviews with seven mental health specialists to ascertain essential biomarkers for the diagnosis of bipolar illness, encompassing HRV, inflammatory markers, oxidative stress markers, genetic markers, neuroimaging alterations, and lifestyle factors. Thematic analysis of the interviews yielded insights into the application of biomarkers in clinical practice and guided recommendations for a digital system that integrates various biomarkers to enhance diagnostic accuracy and patient involvement.

This work underscores the constraints of existing BD diagnostic techniques, which predominantly depend on subjective symptom evaluations. Through consultations with clinicians, we investigate the potential of merging biological and behavioural markers with digital tools to enhance the early detection and management of bipolar disorder. We identify critical indicators, including heart rate variability, inflammatory markers, oxidative stress markers, genetic markers, neuroimaging alterations, and patient engagement measures, and delineate fundamental characteristics for novel diagnostic instruments. These innovations seek to improve diagnostic accuracy, allowing clinicians to make more precise and quicker judgments, hence enhancing patient outcomes. In conclusion, we present the following contributions to this study:

1. We introduce a holistic framework integrating biological, behavioral, and psychosocial factors to enhance BD management through advanced technologies.
2. We explore how technology—like AI monitoring, wearables, and gamified apps can improve BD diagnosis and management.
3. Through clinician interviews, we analyze their expectations and preferences for BD diagnostic tools.
4. We identify essential biomarker measures and patient engagement data that can be incorporated into digital diagnostic tools for BD.
5. We highlight key design aspects for digital health tools to boost diagnostic accuracy, improve patient outcomes, and address BD differentiation challenges.

2   Related Work

The diagnosis of bipolar disorder (BD) has conventionally depended on subjective clinical evaluations according to DSM-5 and ICD criteria. Although these guidelines offer a framework, their reliance on clinician observations and patient self-reports frequently results in misdiagnosis, especially in differentiating bipolar disorder from unipolar depression [5,10,31]. Diagnostic delays may lead to years of unsuitable treatment prior to the establishment of an accurate BD diagnosis [7,9].

To mitigate these limitations, researchers have investigated biomarkers including heart rate variability (HRV), cortisol levels, and neuroimaging data, which provide objective insights into the physiological foundations of mood dysregulation in bipolar disorder (BD) [19,25,33]. Nonetheless, despite their promise, these biomarkers have experienced sluggish clinical adoption owing to difficulties in their integration into current diagnostic frameworks and the intricacy of amalgamating multiple indicators into a cohesive instrument [5,8, 16,35]. Recent advancements in digital health technologies, particularly wearable devices, facilitate continuous monitoring of behavioural and physiological indicators, including sleep patterns, physical activity, and social interactions, all pertinent to the management of bipolar disorder. Mobile health applications augment long-term monitoring and intervention by integrating real-time data with clinical evaluations [15]. Nonetheless, inadequate integration into clinical processes and insufficient clinician participation in tool development continue to pose substantial obstacles to widespread use [11,28]. Research indicates that clinician-centered design, which integrates iterative feedback from physicians, enhances tool use and acceptance [12,17,20].

Machine learning (ML) methodologies, especially those employing neuroimaging and cognitive evaluations, have demonstrated significant accuracy in differentiating BD from healthy controls [6,24]. Nonetheless, numerous ML models neglect to consider clinical variability, hence constraining their practical usefulness in real-world scenarios [23,26]. Addressing this disparity necessitates diagnostic frameworks that integrate biomarkers, digital phenotyping, and clinical experience to guarantee both scientific rigour and practical applicability.

Our project tackles these problems by creating a clinician-focused diagnostic instrument that incorporates biological and behavioural indicators, facilitating smooth integration into clinical practice and enhancing diagnostic accuracy.

3   Method

This project aims to investigate the significance of biomarker measures. To examine the importance of biomarker assessments in diagnosing and treating BD, we performed semi-structured interviews with seven mental health professionals. The interviews sought to comprehend existing diagnostic methods, encountered problems, and anticipations for forthcoming diagnostic instruments. Experts specialising in the diagnosis and treatment of BD were requested to contemplate their experiences, pinpoint essential biomarkers, and propose enhancements for digital health systems. This qualitative methodology offered insights into the incorporation of biomarkers into diagnostic frameworks to improve accuracy and efficiency.

3.1   Interview Study

Clinicians. Seven mental health professionals engaged in this study, concentrating on the diagnosis, treatment, and management of bipolar disorder (BD). These clinicians, who also conduct pertinent research, offered insights into critical biomarkers and the constraints of existing diagnostic techniques. Their expertise was essential in determining how biomarker parameters could enhance diagnostic precision and patient outcomes. The study sought to ascertain their expectations for forthcoming digital health technology to improve diagnostic tools. Our study included seven clinicians, a limited sample size for quantitative research yet appropriate for qualitative research. We prioritised comprehensive insights over quantity, in accordance with Burawoy's focus on deriving profound understanding from a restricted number of examples [34]. We concentrated on professionals possessing practical expertise in BD diagnosis and treatment, as well as a receptiveness to innovative technology. Data saturation was attained by uniform experiences and discoveries concerning biomarkers and diagnostic instruments (Table 1).

Table 1. Clinicians' Information.

ID	Specialization	Experience (years)	BD Patients/Week
C01	Psychiatry	6	5
C02	General Medicine	5	5
C03	Psychiatry	6	4
C04	Psychiatry	4	5
C05	Psychiatry	5	7
C06	Neurology	6	6
C07	General Medicine	3	4

Procedure. Interviews were conducted from May 12 to August 27, 2024, using a semi-structured approach. Questions focused on:

1. Current Processes and Challenges: Steps and challenges in detecting and diagnosing BD.
2. Key Symptoms and Monitoring: Symptoms, lifestyle factors, and current monitoring techniques.
3. Technological Integration: Potential of AI and biomarker tools in clinical practice.
4. Advice for Researchers: Expert opinions on technology-based solutions and biomarker potential.

3.2   Data Analysis

Thematic analysis was performed utilising both inductive and deductive coding methodologies. The inductive phase facilitated the organic emergence of patterns and themes from the data, directly recording physicians' insights. The deductive phase subsequently employed existing ideas to systematically analyse these themes. This dual methodology integrated empirical data with theoretical classification, resulting in a thorough comprehension. Sub-themes were derived from distinct codes, which were subsequently synthesised into principal themes [2] (Table 2).

Table 2. Main Themes in Research.

Main Theme	Description
Current Process and Challenges	It highlights the specific challenges they face in their day-to-day work.
Exploring Psychologist-Applied Biomarker Parameters	Using biomarkers in clinical practice for mental health assessment.
Prototype	Design and functionality suggestions for diagnostic prototypes

4   Results

4.1   Current Assessment Process of BD

A complete medical history, psychiatric symptoms, and family mental health history are needed to diagnose bipolar disorder. Clinicians can diagnose manic and depressive episodes by understanding their cyclical character. "Mood swings are crucial for identifying behavioural changes", said a clinician. Evaluations track mood changes over weeks or months to document the disorder's usual variations. "Identifying the pattern of mood episodes is crucial for distinguishing bipolar disorder from other conditions," said another. Clinicians use DSM-5 criteria and diagnostic tools like the YMRS for manic symptoms and the HAM-D for depressive symptoms. They improve clinical observations with quantitative measurements. Structured interviews are needed to collect symptom frequency, duration, and intensity. "Structured interviews facilitate the collection of comprehensive data that may be overlooked in casual discussions," stated a clinician. Obtaining meaningful patient information, especially during manic periods when self-awareness may be low, is difficult. Thus, clinicians commonly use family information to complete their clinical picture. "Patients frequently underreport their manic symptoms, rendering family collateral an essential element of the assessment," said a clinician (C04). Because many symptoms resemble other mental illnesses, notably major depressive disorder, diagnosis is often uncertain. Different symptom presentations, episode strength and duration, comorbid disorders, and social conditions may hinder help-seeking. The symptom overlap between bipolar disorder and other mood disorders makes diagnosis complicated and time-consuming, noted a clinician (C01). Clinical considerations include sleep quality and consistency mood episode symptoms and factors. Diagnostic signs include social disengagement and activity alterations. A coach noted sleep issues often signal a mood disorder. Continuous management monitors therapeutic efficacy and mood episode recurrence. Later assessments include medication efficacy, side effects, emotional symptom stability, functional recovery, and relapse symptoms. Changing treatment regimens and preventing relapses require regular follow-ups, noted one clinician (C07).

4.2   Parameters Used

Biological and Behavioral Markers: Clinicians acknowledge physiological and behavioural indicators as crucial to understanding and treating BD. Clinicians use HRV and EDA to predict stress and mood swings in bipolar disorder (BD). "HRV is a key indicator of autonomic nervous system dysfunction and mood instability," (C01). HRV shows autonomic nervous system function and aids mood assessment. To reduce false positives in AI-based risk classification, clinicians emphasise its importance in combination with sleep and exercise. "Declines in HRV frequently precede manic episodes; however, contextual factors—such as sleep disturbances—are crucial to validate the trend," noted another clinician (C03). Electrodermal activity patterns are crucial as they signify fluctuations in emotional arousal and can enable early intervention. "Electrodermal reactivity may signify an impending manic episode, facilitating prompt intervention," asserted a clinician (C04). Besides physiological markers, lifestyle factors, especially sleep patterns, are also examined. One clinician said, "Sleep disturbances often serve as the initial indicator of a mood episode and are essential in mood regulation." Clinicians assess sleep quality and consistency as mood episode symptoms and causes. Wearables and smart mattresses with advanced sensors can monitor sleep. Physical activity and nutrition change significantly. "Variations in activity levels and appetite frequently precede mood alterations and serve as critical indicators for early intervention," said another clinician (C05). Clinicians say hunger and activity changes can indicate mood disorders. Key diagnostic signs are activity changes and social disengagement. "Social withdrawal is a significant predictor of an approaching depressive episode, whereas heightened social engagement may indicate mania," said a clinician (C06). Wearable and digital health instruments provide crucial factors for establishing effective BD monitoring and intervention strategies.

Wearable APIs allow real-time physiological data integration into clinical dashboards or AI systems. Clinicians stressed the need for EHR integration and protected cloud pipelines to protect data. Comfort, especially during continuous use, was emphasised, with lighter, less noticeable gadgets receiving more praise. To reduce patient burden and improve adherence, passive sensing and automated synchronisation devices are preferred.

Table 3. Biological, Behavioral, and Psychosocial Factors in Mental Health Assessment

Category	Subcategory	Description
Biological and Behavioral	Physiological Markers	HRV, EDA
	Emotional Symptoms	Dysregulation, mood fluctuations
	Cognitive Changes	Memory issues, impulsivity, risky behaviors
	Physical Symptoms	Sleep/appetite disturbances, activity changes
	Risk Behaviors	Self-harm, suicidality
	Lifestyle Factors	Nutrition, physical activity
Psychosocial	Social Support	Positive interactions, family involvement
	Social Challenges	Isolation, negative interactions
	Behavioral Patterns	Social withdrawal/ over-engagement
	Therapeutic Support	Therapy, support groups
	Family History	Genetic predisposition, psychiatric history
	Caregiver Role	Monitoring mood changes

Psychosocial Factors and Relationships: Effective business development management requires psychosocial and interpersonal considerations. Clinicians say family and close social networks are essential for mood stability and symptom management. Stabilising mood and managing symptoms require social support, especially from family and close friends. Isolation can worsen a patient's condition, yet strong social interactions improve outcomes. Positive social contacts help regulate mood, says a clinician (C01). In contrast, negative social contact and seclusion can worsen symptoms, especially during depression. Depression is exacerbated by negative social interactions and isolation. Adverse social encounters might cause mood swings. (C02). Changes in social behaviour and engagement indicate mood swings. Increased social involvement often precedes manic episodes, while social retreat usually precedes depression. Depression is often accompanied by social disengagement (C03). Depression often leads to suicide thoughts and self-harm. Suicidal thoughts is widespread during depressive episodes, requiring close monitoring and management (C03). Therapeutic interactions and ongoing therapy provide mood regulation tools. "Therapeutic relationships provide consistent support and direction" (C02). Family and caretakers must monitor mood swings and provide emotional support. "Family members observe the patient's mood and behavior" (C02). Finally, familial and medical history are needed to diagnose bipolar disorder, which may be inherited. Understanding familial mental health provides valuable insights (C05,

C03). Therapeutic therapies for bipolar disorder must include psychosocial factors (Table 3).

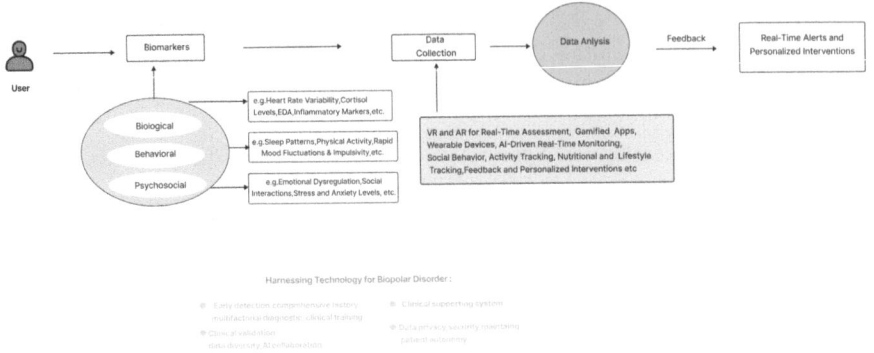

Fig. 1. Framework for managing BD using integrated biomarkers.

4.3 Harnessing Technology for BD Management: Ethical, Clinical, and Research Guidance from Clinicians

This section outlines the findings from our discussions with clinicians regarding technology-based strategies for BD management. Three primary conclusions emerged: notable biomarkers and metrics for monitoring BD, ethical implications of technology, and suggestions for researchers. We propose a framework entitled "Harnessing Technology for BD Management" to integrate these findings, highlighting the collection and analysis of biological, behavioural, and psychological data to provide personalised treatments while ensuring clinical validation, data protection, and compliance with ethical standards. Clinicians expressed substantial ethical apprehensions over the utilisation of AI and technology in the monitoring of bipolar disorder. They underscored the significance of patient permission, data security, and privacy, highlighting that patients must comprehend the methods of data collection, storage, and use. A clinician asserted, "Patients must comprehend the utilisation of their data and possess control over it" (C02). They emphasised the peril of algorithmic bias, observing that AI models trained on unrepresentative datasets may intensify health inequities. "It is imperative to validate AI models across diverse demographics to ensure equity," asserted another clinician (C05). Concerns regarding the prolonged exploitation of data, including unauthorised access by third parties, were expressed. Clinicians advocated for comprehensive data governance frameworks featuring transparent consent processes and patient data control to resolve these challenges. They proposed employing federated learning and edge AI to improve privacy and ensure compliance with legislation like as GDPR and HIPAA. "Incorporating ethics into system design from the outset is essential for patient-centered and socially responsible care," stated a physician (C07) (Fig. 1).

Essential Metrics for Monitoring Bipolar Disorder and Framework:
Clinicians stressed bipolar disorder monitoring requirements. HRV and GSR are crucial mood indicators. HRV and GSR can predict mood episodes, according to a clinician (C01). Wearable gear enhances quick detection. Sleep abnormalities like hypersomnia in depression and sleeplessness in mania are important markers. A clinician (C04) said, "Monitoring sleep patterns is crucial for predicting mood fluctuations." Wearables and smart mattresses with advanced sensors track sleep. Changes in diet and exercise are significant. Clinicians recognised that appetite and activity changes can indicate mood episodes (C05, C06). A neuro-behavioral feedback apparatus uses real-time neuroimaging and behavioral monitoring to deliver comprehensive insights. Emotional instability and impulsivity are equally important. Passive digital surveillance, including smartphone use and physical activity, helps identify behavioural anomalies. Treatment must address melatonin and circadian rhythm disorders. Melatonin and circadian rhythm monitoring are needed to stabilise bipolar disorder mood. Wearables and smart mattresses can track sleep and melatonin. Cognitive tests and financial monitoring can spot risky behaviour. Early mood episode detection requires monitoring oxidative stress and inflammatory indicators. Social behaviour can reveal mood swings early. Hunger, weight, and diet affect mood. Holistic care treats anxiety and substance misuse. Entertainment computing enhances diagnosis.

Guidance for Researchers: To guarantee the efficacy of technology-driven solutions for BD monitoring and therapy, researchers must prioritise clinical validation. A physician asserted, "Prototypes necessitate comprehensive clinical validation." (C02). The multivariate data collection approach enhances precision. We propose a hybrid AI architecture that integrates long short-term memory (LSTM) networks for analysing sequential physiological signals (e.g., HRV, sleep, electrodermal activity) with dense feedforward layers for structured behavioural and self-reported data (e.g., social activity, mood logs). Data from several modalities are amalgamated using a late fusion technique employing a multi-head attention mechanism, allowing the model to assess and prioritise inputs according to their predictive significance for mood state transitions. Real-time inference is enabled by APIs integrated into wearable devices that transmit encrypted data to a cloud-based processing layer, which then provides risk scores and trend summaries to clinicians through a dashboard. Artificial intelligence should assist clinicians in decision-making without supplanting human competence. Usability, accessibility, and patient-centred design are essential for effective therapeutic interventions. Moreover, prioritising adaptability is essential to facilitate modifications informed by clinical feedback. A thorough symptom analysis across several data points substantiates any technology-driven intervention for BD.

5   Discussion

This study investigated the difficulties clinicians encounter in identifying bipolar disorder and how the incorporation of biomarker characteristics with computerised diagnostic tools can improve accuracy and treatment strategies.

Biomarker Integration for Diagnosis: Our research indicates that integrating essential biomarker traits into bipolar disorder diagnostic algorithms markedly enhances diagnostic precision and facilitates more individualised treatment. Clinicians recognised physiological indicators such as HRV, cortisol concentrations, and sleep patterns as essential data points, in addition to behavioural markers. This integration facilitates data-driven, real-time therapeutic decisions. These findings correspond with increasing studies endorsing the utilisation of objective physiological data in mental health diagnosis, namely heart rate variability as an indicator of mood instability [21,32]. Biomarkers address the shortcomings of conventional techniques reliant on patient self-reports and professional observations. According to Perochon S (2023) and Boukarras S (2024), clinicians can identify mood fluctuations earlier and execute prompt therapies by observing physiological indicators in conjunction with behavioural alterations [4,30]. Behavioural indicators, including alterations in physical activity and sleep patterns, serve as critical early warning signs of mood instability. Observing sleep patterns yields insights on the emergence of manic and depressive episodes. The integration of behavioural and biological markers assists clinicians in addressing the unpredictability of bipolar disorder symptoms. In conclusion, the amalgamation of behavioural and biological markers into a unified diagnostic framework offers a more methodical and objective method for detecting bipolar disease. This allows clinicians to expedite and customise treatment decisions through a data-driven approach [36,38].

Current Diagnostic Challenges: Clinicians continue to have difficulties in diagnosing bipolar disorder, especially in distinguishing it from other mood disorders such as unipolar depression. The symptom overlap frequently results in misdiagnosis, with patients exhibiting analogous depressive symptoms in both contexts. Manic or hypomanic episodes, critical characteristics of bipolar disorder, are frequently concealed or underreported by patients. This may hinder physicians' ability to identify the complete range of BD symptoms. The patient's condition may deteriorate, and long-term care may become increasingly challenging due to this misdiagnosis, perhaps delaying necessary treatment for years. BD is challenging to diagnose due to the extensive variability in symptom presentation. Marked variations in mood, activity, and behaviour are characteristic of bipolar disorder. Some individuals may see intense, rapid mood fluctuations, whereas others endure significant periods between episodes. BD is frequently misinterpreted as unipolar depression or other mood disorders due to its initial presentation of milder or atypical symptoms. Further impediments to precise diagnosis encompass cultural stigma and patient hesitance to reveal symptoms. This hesitation may hinder clinicians from obtaining a comprehensive understanding of the patient's mood fluctuations, resulting in erroneous or inadequate evaluations.

Understanding Clinicians' Anticipations for Diagnostic Instruments: Clinicians identified essential criteria for diagnostic tools utilised in the treatment of BD, highlighting the need for systems that enable real-time monitoring, provide longitudinal data, and can be customised to meet individual patient requirements. Given the variable nature of bipolar disorder, physicians highlighted the importance of sleep patterns and HRV as essential physiological indicators for tracking sudden mood changes. The integration of wearable technologies was emphasised as a primary expectation. Wearable sensors provide the advantage of continuous, remote monitoring of physiological data, including heart rate variability, physical activity, and sleep patterns. The capacity to remotely gather data facilitates prompt modifications to medication or therapy according to current patient metrics, hence improving treatment efficacy. The advancement of AI-driven diagnostic tools raises significant ethical concerns, especially with patient autonomy and data privacy. Clarity concerning the collection, retention, and utilisation of patient data is crucial. Clinicians articulated a significant expectation for the personalisation of diagnostic instruments. Given that each patient with BD exhibits distinct characteristics, tools must be tailored to address the individual requirements and situations of each person. Clinicians anticipate the integration of advanced technical components, such as wearable devices and real-time monitoring, with ethical measures to uphold patient autonomy and privacy in bipolar disorder diagnostic tools.

Designing a Clinician-Centered Diagnostic Prototype: The outcomes of this study emphasise that an effective clinician-centered diagnostic prototype for BD must integrate behavioural and biological indicators, facilitate real-time data processing, and provide an intuitive user interface. The physicians participating in the study underscored that the development of diagnostic tools should augment their clinical practices rather than interfere with them. The amalgamation of wearable technologies with AI platforms to assess both objective and subjective data is a crucial component of the proposed prototype. The technology allows clinicians to remotely and simultaneously monitor patients by continuously collecting real-time physiological data. The diagnostic prototype's effectiveness would improve by integrating decision-support tools that provide actionable insights based on real-time data trends. Ensuring the interface is intuitive and user-friendly for physicians is a critical component of the prototype's design. Furthermore, a crucial characteristic that practitioners desire in diagnostic tools is customisation. The prototype must offer individualised monitoring tailored to each patient's specific needs. In summary, an effective clinician-centered diagnostic prototype should incorporate wearable technology for continuous data collection, real-time monitoring of behavioural and physiological variables, and decision-support tools that provide actionable insights while preserving physician autonomy.

6   Limitations and Future Directions

This study possesses some shortcomings that warrant acknowledgement. The limited sample size (N = 7 clinicians) constrains the generalizability of the findings, and the absence of patient data from varied demographics raises concerns regarding broader application. Secondly, although the proposed biomarker integration system demonstrates potential, it necessitates validation in actual clinical environments. Third, significant ethical concerns around data protection and AI interpretability were not thoroughly examined. Future research should: (1) encompass larger, more heterogeneous samples comprising both clinicians and patients across various healthcare environments; (2) implement clinical trials to substantiate the efficacy of the diagnostic framework; and (3) examine essential ethical considerations, including data protection measures and patient consent procedures. Moreover, tailoring these tools to diverse cultural and socioeconomic situations will be crucial for equitable execution.

7   Conclusion

Bipolar disorder (BD) diagnosis using biomarker assessments and clinicians' hopes for future tools are examined in this study. Specialist interviews revealed physiological and behavioural signs that could improve diagnosis. The findings demonstrate the need for data-driven, real-time monitoring solutions that connect with clinical procedures and provide personalised insights.

Use an integrated biomarker-clinical framework, wearable tech for continuous monitoring, and AI-driven decision support to overcome diagnostic limits. We found that clinician-centered technologies increase BD detection precision and timing, enabling early intervention. These findings can improve biomarker efficacy in minimising misdiagnosis and improving patient outcomes in clinician-specific digital health systems. For successful acceptance, future research should focus on clinical validation, data privacy, and practical implementation. Using objective biomarkers and clinical evaluations could improve BD diagnosis, therapy, and long-term care.

References

1. Abi-Dargham, A., et al.: Candidate biomarkers in psychiatric disorders: state of the field. World Psychiatry **22**(2), 236–262 (2023). https://doi.org/10.1002/wps.21078
2. Bauer, M., et al.: Smartphones in mental health: a critical review of background issues, current status and future concerns. Int. J. Bipolar Disord. **8**(1), 1–19 (2020). https://doi.org/10.1186/s40345-019-0164-x
3. Bhatnagar, A., Murray, G., Ray, S.: Circadian biology to advance therapeutics for mood disorders. Trends Pharmacol. Sci. **44**(10), 689–704 (2023). https://doi.org/10.1016/j.tips.2023.07.008

4. Boukarras, S., Ferri, D., Borgogni, L., Aglioti, S.: Neurophysiological markers of asymmetric emotional contagion: implications for organizational contexts. Front. Integr. Neurosci. **18**, 1321130 (2024). https://doi.org/10.3389/fnint.2024.1321130

5. Carvalho, A., Firth, J., Vieta, E.: Bipolar disorder. N. Engl. J. Med. **383**(1), 58–66 (2020). https://doi.org/10.1056/NEJMra1906193

6. Colombo, F., Calesella, F., Mazza, M., et al.: Machine learning approaches for prediction of bipolar disorder based on biological, clinical and neuropsychological markers: a systematic review and meta-analysis. Neurosci. Biobehav. Rev. **135**, 104552 (2022). https://doi.org/10.1016/j.neubiorev.2022.104552

7. De Azevedo Cardoso, T., Kochhar, S., Torous, J., Morton, E.: Digital tools to facilitate the detection and treatment of bipolar disorder: key developments and future directions. JMIR Ment. Health **11**, e58631 (2024). https://doi.org/10.2196/58631

8. De Felice, G., et al.: Can brain-derived neurotrophic factor be considered a biomarker for bipolar disorder? an analysis of the current evidence. Brain Sci. **13**(8), 1221 (2023). https://doi.org/10.3390/brainsci13081221

9. Ersan, S., Cigdem, B., Bakir, D., Dogan, H.: Determination of levels of oxidative stress and nitrosative stress in patients with epilepsy. Epilepsy Res. **164**, 106352 (2020). https://doi.org/10.1016/j.eplepsyres.2020.106352

10. Faurholt-Jepsen, M., et al.: Reducing the rate of psychiatric re-admissions in bipolar disorder using smartphones–the RADMIS trial. Acta Psychiatr. Scand. **143**(5), 453–465 (2021). https://doi.org/10.1111/acps.13274

11. Gomis-Pastor, M., Berdún, J., Borrás-Santos, A., et al.: Clinical validation of digital healthcare solutions: state of the art, challenges and opportunities. Healthcare **12**, 1057 (2024). https://doi.org/10.3390/healthcare12111057

12. Grover, T., Hill, C., Smith, L., et al.: Defining features of patient-centered care: a qualitative analysis. Neurosci. Biobehav. Rev. **139**, 104552 (2022). https://doi.org/10.1016/j.neubiorev.2022.104552

13. Guttal, T.: AI as a communication facilitator: shared decision-making inspired strategies for bipolar disorder diagnosis and treatment (2023). https://doi.org/10.48550/arXiv.2304.07878

14. Hernández-Gómez, A., Andrade-González, N., Lahera, G., Vieta, E.: Recommendations for the care of patients with bipolar disorder during the COVID-19 pandemic. J. Affect. Disord. **279**, 117–121 (2021). https://doi.org/10.1016/j.jad.2020.09.105

15. Hicks, J., Boswell, M., Althoff, T., et al.: Leveraging mobile technology for public health promotion: a multidisciplinary perspective. Annu. Rev. Public Health **44**, 131–150 (2023). https://doi.org/10.1146/annurev-publhealth-060220-041643

16. Jain, A., Mitra, P.: Bipolar disorder. In: StatPearls [Internet]. StatPearls Publishing, Treasure Island (FL) (2025). https://www.ncbi.nlm.nih.gov/books/NBK558998. Accessed 20 Feb 2023

17. Janerka, C., Leslie, G., Gill, F.: Development of patient-centred care in acute hospital settings: a meta-narrative review. Int. J. Nurs. Stud. **140**, 104465 (2023). https://doi.org/10.1016/j.ijnurstu.2023.104465

18. Janssen Daalen, J., et al.: Digital biomarkers for non-motor symptoms in Parkinson's disease: the state of the art. NPJ Digit. Med. **7**(1), 186 (2024). https://doi.org/10.1038/s41746-024-01144-2

19. Kamińska, D., Kamińska, O., Sochacka, M., Sokół-Szawłowska, M.: The role of selected speech signal characteristics in discriminating unipolar and bipolar disorders. Sensors **24**(14), 4721 (2024). https://doi.org/10.3390/s24144721

20. Khatiwada, P., Yang, B., Lin, J., Blobel, B.: Patient-generated health data (PGHD): understanding, requirements, challenges, and existing techniques for data security and privacy. J. Pers. Med. **14**(3), 282 (2024). https://doi.org/10.3390/jpm14030282

21. Kircanski, K., Williams, L., Gotlib, I.: Heart rate variability as a biomarker of anxious depression response to antidepressant medication. Depress. Anxiety **36**(1), 63–71 (2019). https://doi.org/10.1002/da.22843

22. Kirkpatrick, R., Munoz, D., Khalid-Khan, S., Booij, L.: Methodological and clinical challenges associated with biomarkers for psychiatric disease: a scoping review. J. Psychiatr. Res. **143** (2020). https://doi.org/10.1016/j.jpsychires.2020.11.023

23. Kumar, Y., Koul, A., Singla, R., Ijaz, M.F.: Artificial intelligence in disease diagnosis: a systematic literature review, synthesizing framework and future research agenda. J. Ambient. Intell. Humaniz. Comput. (1), 1–28 (2021). https://doi.org/10.1007/s12652-021-03612-z

24. Mikolas, P., Marxen, M., Riedel, P., et al.: Prediction of estimated risk for bipolar disorder using machine learning and structural MRI features. Psychol. Med. **54**(2), 278–288 (2024). https://doi.org/10.1017/S0033291723001319

25. Miller, J.N., Black, D.W.: Bipolar disorder and suicide: a review. Curr. Psychiatry Rep. **22**(2), 1–10 (2020). https://doi.org/10.1007/s11920-020-1130-0

26. Milne, S., Kueh, C., Medley, S., Lynch, N., Noteboom, B.: Human-centered service design and transformative innovation: beginning to understand how innovation culture shifts within the public health system in western Australia. In: Pfannstiel, M. (ed.) Human-Centered Service Design for Healthcare Transformation. Springer, Cham (2023). https://doi.org/10.1007/978-3-031-20168-4

27. Mullins, N., et al.: Genome-wide association study of >40,000 bipolar disorder cases. Nat. Genet. **53**(6), 817–829 (2021). https://doi.org/10.1038/s41588-021-00857-4

28. Borges do Nascimento, I., Abdulazeem, H., Vasanthan, L., et al.: Barriers and facilitators to utilizing digital health technologies by healthcare professionals. NPJ Digit. Med. **6**(1), 161 (2023). https://doi.org/10.1038/s41746-023-00899-4

29. O'Connell, N., et al.: Early intervention in psychosis services: a systematic review and narrative synthesis of the barriers and facilitators to implementation. Eur. Psychiatry **65**(1), e2 (2021). https://doi.org/10.1192/j.eurpsy.2021.2260

30. Perochon, S., et al.: Early detection of autism using digital behavioral phenotyping. Nat. Med. **29**(10), 2489–2497 (2023). https://doi.org/10.1038/s41591-023-02574-3

31. Phillips, M.L., Kupfer, D.J.: Bipolar disorder diagnosis: challenges and future directions. Lancet **381**(9878), 1663–1671 (2013). https://doi.org/10.1016/S0140-6736(13)60989-7

32. Pérez-Ramos, A., Romero-López-Alberca, C., Hidalgo-Figueroa, M., et al.: A systematic review of the biomarkers associated with cognition and mood state in bipolar disorder. Int. J. Bipolar Disord. **12**, 18 (2024). https://doi.org/10.1186/s40345-024-00340-z

33. Shinba, T., et al.: Heart rate variability measurement can be a point-of-care sensing tool for screening postpartum depression: differentiation from adjustment disorder. Sensors **24**(5), 1459 (2024). https://doi.org/10.3390/s24051459

34. Tenny, S., Brannan, J., Brannan, G.: Qualitative study. In: StatPearls [Internet]. StatPearls Publishing (2024). https://www.ncbi.nlm.nih.gov/books/NBK470395/

35. Wang, L., Hu, Y., Jiang, N., Yetisen, A.: Biosensors for psychiatric biomarkers in mental health monitoring. Biosens. Bioelectron. **256**, 116242 (2024). https://doi.org/10.1016/j.bios.2024.116242

36. Williamson, S.: Digital phenotyping in psychiatry. BJPsych. Adv. **29**, 1–2 (2023). https://doi.org/10.1192/bja.2023.26

37. Yatham, L.: Biomarkers for clinical use in psychiatry: where are we and will we ever get there? World Psychiatry **22**(2), 263–264 (2023). https://doi.org/10.1002/wps.21079

38. Yeung, A., Torkamani, A., Butte, A., Glicksberg, B.: Schuller: the promise of digital healthcare technologies. Front. Public Health **11**, 1196596 (2023). https://doi.org/10.3389/fpubh.2023.1196596

Exploring How Generative AI Painting Systems Can Enhance Social Connectedness Between Young Adults and Parents Living Apart

Chenwei Liang[1]([envelope]), Rui Wang[1], Ye Lin[2], Pengcheng An[3], and Jun Hu[1]

[1] Department of Industrial Design, Eindhoven University of Technology, Eindhoven, The Netherlands
{c.liang1,r.wang1,j.hu}@tue.nl
[2] School of Design, Hunan Institute of Engineering, Xiangtan, China
[3] School of Design, Southern University of Science and Technology, Shenzhen, China
anpc@sustech.edu.cn

Abstract. This study explores how generative AI (Gen AI) painting systems can enhance social connectedness between young adults and children who live apart. We designed a system that transforms personal sound recordings, emotional prompts, and photos into visual artworks, and investigated how different levels of parents' related information involvement affect young adults' connectedness with their parents. Through a within-subject pilot study with three participants, we compared three modes of AI-assisted visualization, ranging from different levels of human information involvement based on Gen AI support. Our findings suggest that greater personalization, particularly when incorporating emotionally meaningful photos, can elicit stronger feelings of connection. However, more involvement does not always produce stronger connectedness; effectiveness depends on perceived emotional intent and contextual relevance. We conclude with design implications for future human-AI co-creative systems that aim to foster social connectedness in long-distance families.

Keywords: Social connectedness · Gen AI · Human AI collaboration

1 Introduction

The World Health Organization reports a record high global migrant population, including people who relocate to seek employment or educational opportunities [46]. Such long distance separation challenges emotional bonds and weakens the social connectedness between parents and children [37]. Within human-computer interaction, visualizing personal data through digital art has emerged as a non-intrusive and effective approach to fostering social connectedness [16,23–25,41]. Compared to direct communication tools, generative data-driven artworks allow people to express and perceive emotional cues in subtle

R. Yamanishi et al. (Eds.): ICEC 2025 Workshops, LNCS 15935, pp. 76–91, 2025.
https://doi.org/10.1007/978-3-032-02534-0_9

and aesthetically engaging ways [19,35,47–49]. However, traditional visualization methods that implement personalized design principles are usually costly and relatively unfriendly to the common user [28]. With the rise of Gen AI, creating personalized artworks has become more accessible to the general public [34,50].

This study explores how Gen AI can serve as a supplementary medium to generate low-cost, emotionally expressive, and visually engaging digital artwork that supports social connectedness between geographically separated parents and young adults. Although prior research has investigated the perception and preference for AI- versus human-created works [10,26], and the role of human oversight in improving content acceptance [14,53], the specific impact of different levels of human involvement remains underexplored. To address this gap, we investigate how different involvement levels of parents in AI-generated paintings affect young adults' sense of social connectedness. Our system uses sound data, prompts, and pictures as basic input, which Gen AI analyzes to generate visual output. We define three visualization modes based on existing Gen AI methods [15,43,51]:

Method 1 - (AI + sound data) -AI (50%) + human information (50%): The AI independently processes sound data and generates visual output without human intervention.

Method 2 - (AI + sound data + emotional prompt) - AI (33%) + human information (66%): The AI incorporates sound data and additional human-provided emotional cues to guide the generation.

Method 3 - (AI + sound data + emotional prompt + photo) - AI (25%) + human information (75%): In addition to sound and emotional prompts, a photo is provided to enrich the visual representation collaboratively.

Based on these methods, this study poses the following research question: "How do different involvement levels of parents in AI-generated painting affect the social connectedness between young adults and their parents who live apart?" In essence, we seek to understand how increasing parents' information involvement in generative AI art influences young adults' emotional perceptions and young adults' feelings of connectedness in long-distance parent-young adults relationships.

2   Related Work

2.1   Social Connectedness

Social connectedness refers to the degree to which individuals perceive a sense of connection, belonging, and emotional bond with others or groups. It emphasizes emotional interactions, communication, and mutual support between people. This connection promotes psychological satisfaction, a sense of security, and general well-being [4,7–9,17,45]. Social connectedness can be described in a hierarchy of three tiers: the most intimate tier includes close family members, the next tier comprises close friends and acquaintances, and the outermost tier involves strangers with whom one interacts [39]. Previous research has shown that a strong sense of positive social connectedness primarily emerges within the context of mutual care and understanding, specifically among the most intimate relationships such as family members and partners [3,39].

2.2 Emerging Technologies to Support Social Connectedness

Many early systems have been designed to support social connectedness among remote family members. For example, ambient displays of 'awareness' such as Digital Family Portrait [30] and CareNet [5] shared an elder's daily routine with distant relatives, providing peace of mind while respecting the elder's privacy. Other devices enabled lightweight emotional exchanges: the Lovelet wearable communicated the warmth of a loved one [13], and eKiss allowed parents and children to exchange virtual 'kisses' through synchronized photos [6]. Even simple digital 'sticky note' interfaces let family members leave casual messages on shared devices or family websites [31]. More creative approaches have also been explored, such as shared storytelling activities for geographically separated loved ones [22]. All of these efforts aimed to cultivate a sense of closeness and mutual awareness in everyday life despite physical separation. However, while such systems foster peripheral awareness and playful interaction, they generally rely on static content or pre-defined modes of communication. Interactions are often one-directional or limited to preset messages, making it difficult to convey nuanced emotions or adapt to the changing context of an individual [9]. Furthermore, these systems often require high costs to create and maintain digital visualizations, making it difficult to achieve scalable personalization [28]. Generative AI techniques can dynamically tailor content and responses to the situation of a user, potentially infusing exchanges with greater personalization and emotional resonance than was possible with earlier static designs [54]. For example, an AI-driven system can dynamically align content and visualizations with the evolving emotional states and personal preferences of a family member based on real-time analysis of voice signals or text input.

Importantly, Gen AI also offers the potential to create personalized visualizations at a significantly lower cost compared to traditional manual design processes [2]. By automating aspects of content creation and optimization, AI can reduce the burden of manual curation while dynamically adapting to users' evolving emotional and contextual needs. Through the interpretation of multimodal inputs, such as voice tone, textual sentiment, or shared images, AI systems can help identify underlying emotional cues and selectively amplify meaningful signals [11]. This enables not only more personalized communication, but also more effective transmission of emotional intent across distance. In particular, the goal of introducing AI in this context is to support and personalize human-to-human communication rather than to replace it. By acting as a behind-the-scenes facilitator, generative AI can help remote family interactions feel more emotionally attuned and personalized, while keeping the focus on family members and their shared experiences.

2.3   Human Involvement and Emotional Value of AI-Created Works

Existing Gen AI research has focused predominantly on comparing people's emotional responses to human-created content versus AI-generated content, often examining the perceived value and acceptance of each [12,42]. In domains ranging from text and music to visual art, many studies report a bias favoring human-made creations [10,12]. For example, Ragot et al. [29] found that participants rated artworks believed to be human-created significantly higher than those labeled AI-generated. However, when the true origin of a piece is concealed, this preference can diminish or even reverse - some audiences have shown equal or greater appreciation for AI-generated works under blind conditions [29,53]. Such findings highlight a complex public attitude: while there is skepticism toward art known to be made with AI, people may still find AI creations compelling when evaluated on their intrinsic merits alone [42].

Researchers have also explored how the creation process, particularly the level of human involvement, influences the creators' and viewers' perceptions of AI-assisted works. For example, Draxler et al. [10] reported that when users retained greater control over an AI-supported writing task, their sense of ownership over the resulting content increased. This suggests that a creator's active involvement (e.g., guiding the AI or making creative decisions) can strengthen their emotional attachment and the feeling of leadership toward the output. Similarly, in the context of visual art, moderate human guidance in the generative process has been shown to improve audience evaluations of the creativity and quality of the artwork, while excessive reliance on automation can undermine its perceived value [27]. In other words, a balanced human-AI collaboration tends to yield the most positively perceived outcomes.

Beyond the creators themselves, the degree of human involvement can also shape the perception of the audience of the finished work. Zhang et al. [53] investigated how knowing the source of the creation influences viewers' judgments about AI-generated art. They observed a clear 'human preference' effect: Participants gave higher ratings to pieces they were told had been created by a person, yet when they were unaware of an artwork's origin, they often favored the AI-generated version. In particular, Zhang and colleagues further posited that visible human supervision or input during an AI's creative process can elevate an audience's appreciation of the result.

Although these previous studies provide important insights, most have examined emotional responses to AI-generated content in settings where the creator and the audience are unconnected or anonymous and have not explored deeply how different levels of human involvement affect the perception of such works. In contrast, our study focuses on creative works exchanged within relationships between close family members, specifically between parents and young adults. We investigate how different involvement levels of parents in an AI-driven creative process influence not only the young adults' emotional perception of the resulting artwork but also the extent to which such involvement enhances social connectedness between parents and young adults living apart. By highlighting this overlooked relational context, our work explores how human-AI collaboration can enhance not only the perceived value of the Gen AI artwork itself but also the social connectedness between people who share an intimate bond.

3   Final Design and Implementation

The inspiration for this study comes from previous research findings of other researchers that human participation influences the perceived value of AI-generated work by users [10, 26, 53]. This study aims to extend this insight by exploring how different levels of human involvement in an AI-driven creative process affect social connectedness between family members. This section introduces design considerations. To ground the generative process in the lived experiences of users, we selected raw sound data as the primary input. The sound is vivid and expressive, often reflecting an individual's daily routines and emotional states authentically [20]. It carries various types of information, including emotional and behavioral cues embedded in everyday contexts [52]. Previous work has shown that key sound features-such as frequency, loudness, and duration, can effectively reveal aspects of a person's activity or environment [21]. Based on these insights, we utilize GPT-4o's audio analysis capabilities to extract and interpret these features as the basis for generating personalized visual artwork.

3.1   Visual Mapping Mechanism

To ensure consistency and coherence in AI-generated paintings and to control experimental variables, the design principles of generative AI [44] played a crucial role. We developed dedicated GPT models in the GPT Store and established a set of mapping rules to translate sound features, emotion prompts, and pictures provided by parents into visual elements:

- **Sound frequency** determines the number of birds in the artwork;
- **Sound duration** influences the complexity and richness of the image;
- **Sound loudness** reflects the height and quantity of trees and mountains;
- **Sound variability** is mapped to the intensity and movement of water waves.

Using this rule-based mapping, the system dynamically transforms personal sound data into visual graphics. The intention is that the resulting AI-generated image encodes subtle details of the sound. Family members viewing the image can infer cues about the recorder's context or emotions - for example, an AI image with many birds and tall trees could reflect a lively, loud environment, providing a window into each other's daily life. This artistic translation from sound to imagery is designed to foster emotional closeness and strengthen connections through a shared creative experience.

3.2   Visualization Methods

To further investigate the role of human involvement, we created three distinct visualization modes that progressively increase the level of user participation in the generation process (Fig. 1). All three modes use the same sound-to-visual mapping rules defined above, ensuring that the outcomes are comparable while varying the degree of human input. By examining these modes side by side, we can isolate the impact of additional user contributions on the artwork and on the sense of social connectedness. The three generative modes are the following.

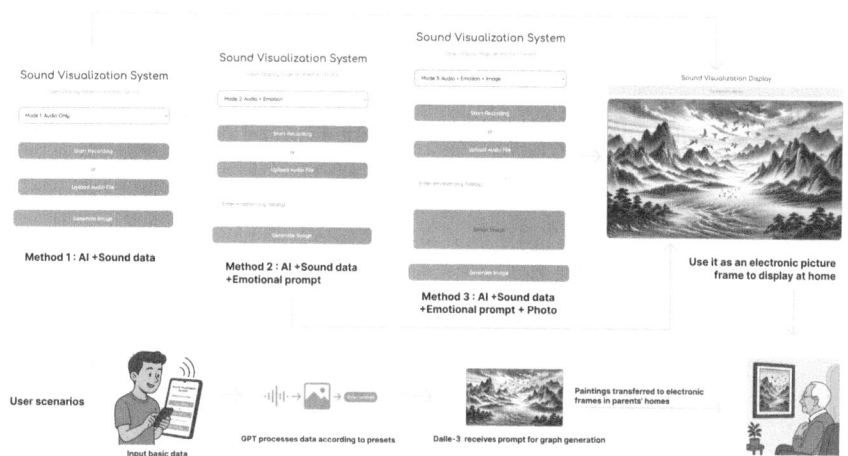

Fig. 1. This diagram illustrates a multimodal visualization pipeline using sound data, emotional prompts, and optional photos to generate personalized images for remote emotional expression. The two cartoon-style illustrations (bottom-left and bottom-right) were generated using GPT-4o to depict user interaction and home display scenarios

- **Method 1 (AI + sound data) - AI (50%) + human information (50%):**
  In this baseline mode, images are generated solely from the sound data using the predefined mapping rules, without additional input from the user. The process is fully automated by AI: the system analyzes raw audio and directly produces a visual output based on these sound features. This mode represents the case of minimal human involvement, where the user's role is only to provide the initial audio recording.
- **Method 2 (AI + sound data + emotional prompt) - AI (33%) + human information (66%):**
  In this mode, the user provides a brief emotional prompt alongside the sound input to guide image generation. The prompt, a word or short phrase such as 'happy' or 'lonely', is used to convey an intended emotional tone. The GPT-4o agent of the system analyzes the sound features while simultaneously adjusting the visual output based on the emotional context. This not only influences the mood of the generated image, but also affects its overall color palette and

stylistic direction. By blending objective audio cues with subjective emotional input, this method introduces a moderate level of human guidance into the creative process.

– **Method 3 (AI + sound data + emotional prompt + photo) - AI (25%) + human information (75%):**
This mode represents the highest level of human information involvement, incorporating an emotional prompt and a reference photo in addition to the sound input. The photo-such as one recently taken by the parent-provides visual cues that guide the generation process. The GPT-4o model extracts key elements from the image, such as people or meaningful objects, and integrates them with the audio features and emotional prompt. This fusion of all three inputs results in a highly personalized and emotionally resonant visual output (Fig 2).

Method 1 (AI + sound data) -AI (50%) + human informa-
tion (50%)   Method 2 (AI + sound data + emotional prompt) - AI (33%)
+human information (66%)   Method 3 (AI + sound data + emotional prompt + photo) -
AI(25%) + human information (75%)human information
(66%)

Fig. 2. AI-Generated Visualizations Using Method 1, 2, and 3

By progressively increasing parents' information involvement in the AI-generated art process, the study seeks to gain insights into how the intervention pf parents affects a young adult's perceived value of AI-generated work, as well as the impact on the social connectedness between young adults and their parents living apart.

4   User Study

This study conducted a pilot study to examine how different levels of related information involvement of parents in generative AI visualization affect social connectedness between young adults and their parents living apart. Three unmarried participants (1 female, 2 males; M = 24) who had lived apart from their parents for at least three months were recruited. The study used a within-subject design with three visualization conditions, each reflecting a distinct level of the involvement of parents. Parents provided audio recordings, emotional prompts, and a photo, which were used to generate images via ChatGPT-4o. Participants received images and contextual information three times a day over 24 h per condition. The order of the conditions was randomized, and a 48-hour interval was applied between sessions to avoid carryover effects. To measure social connectedness and attitudes toward AI, participants completed the Inclusion of Other in the Self Scale (IOS scale) [1] before and after each condition and the General Attitudes towards Artificial Intelligence Scale (GAAIS) [32,33] at the beginning. A manipulation check based on the work of Draxler et al. [10] assessed perceived involvement of parents. After each condition, a semi-structured interview was conducted. When the participants had experienced all the methods, a summative interview was conducted. As the study focuses on the lived experience of users, we applied interpretative phenomenological analysis [38] to explore how different visualization methods shaped emotional perception and social connectedness.

5   Results

5.1   Quantitative Data

Due to the limited sample size, this study has not opted to perform a complete quantitative analysis. However, we will present the quantitative data results from the existing GAAIS and IOS scales and qualitative data. The results of the manipulation test require a larger dataset to ensure statistical validity and, as such, will not be included in this paper.

GAAIS Results. The GAAIS was used to evaluate participants' attitudes toward AI, consisting of both positive and negative subscales. Higher scores on each subscale indicate a more positive attitude; in particular, a high score on the negative subscale reflects greater tolerance for the potential drawbacks of AI. The results show that Participant 1 (P1) had a positive subscale mean of 3.75 and a negative subscale mean of 2.625; Participant 2 (P2) scored 3.92 on the positive subscale and 2.88 on the negative; and Participant 3 (P3) scored 3.75 and 2.5 on the positive and negative subscales, respectively. All participants scored within the moderate range on the positive subscale (3.75–3.92), indicating generally favorable attitudes toward AI. However, the negative subscale revealed a greater variation in the tolerance for the limitations of AI, with P3 showing the lowest tolerance (2.5) and P2 the highest (2.88) (Table 1).

IOS Scale Results. To evaluate the effectiveness of the three visualization methods (Method 1, Method 2, and Method 3) in enhancing social connectedness, we analyzed changes in participants' IOS scores before and after each condition. Only Participants 2 and 3 experienced an increase in social connectedness following Method 3, while Participant 1 did not show any change across all methods. The average change in IOS scores for each method is summarized in Fig. 3, with Method 1 and Method 2 both showing no change (0.0), and Method 3 showing an average increase of +1.0. Although Method 3 appears to produce a positive effect, the limited sample size prevents any statistical inference, and the result is interpreted only as a preliminary trend.

Table 1. GAAIS subscale scores for each participant. Higher positive subscale scores indicate favorable attitudes toward AI; higher negative subscale scores reflect greater tolerance of AI limitations.

Subscale	P1	P2	P3	Mean	Max	Min
Positive Subscale	3.75	3.92	3.75	3.81	3.92	3.75
Negative Subscale	2.63	2.88	2.50	2.67	2.88	2.50

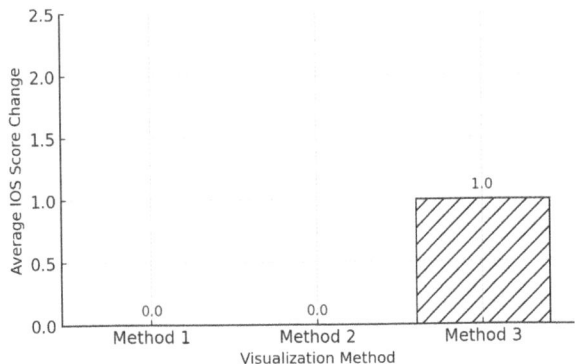

Fig. 3. Average IOS score change by three visualization methods

5.2   Qualitative Data

Low Level Involvement of Parent and Weak Emotional Triggers. Across participants, AI-generated images in Method 1 (sound only) and Method 2 (sound with emotion prompt) were consistently perceived as abstract, impersonal and lacking emotional resonance. P1 commented, "There is no sense of connection because this doesn't feel like my mom's style at all," further explaining that the images "didn't remind me of anything related to my mother. It's just an image." Similarly, P3 remarked, "It feels like random audio data was used to generate something and labelled as my mom's. There's nothing concrete that represents my parents."

Even when emotional prompts were added in Method 2, participants found the expressive power of the images limited. Some minor cues, such as 'sunlight', were occasionally linked to mood, but the connection remained weak. As P1 noted, "The sunlight made me feel like it might correspond to her mood a little, but the change wasn't obvious." P2 echoed this by stating that although the sunshine "helped a bit," the overall experience still felt "too AI-driven" and failed to evoke personal memories. Participants generally agreed that AI dominated the generation process, while the involvement of parents was minimal, resulting in a sense of disconnection.

Personalized Visuals and Perceived Connection. In Method 3, which incorporated the photos of parents along with audio and prompts, the participants reported a noticeably stronger sense of social connection. When the generated image included concrete, relatable elements, especially human figures or familiar settings, participants described emotional responses and a perceived sense of intentional communication from their parents.

P1 reflected, "The part with people is definitely the most important because it directly reflects my mom's actions. There's a story now-people and relationships." P3 similarly commented, "Seeing that person standing there, I immediately felt like it was a photo my mom took and sent to me. It felt like communication." These responses illustrate how personalized visual content enhances narrative coherence and fosters a feeling of relational presence.

However, the positive effect of Method 3 was not universal. P2 noted that although the image included the input from parents, it still failed to resonate: "This kind of photo could come from anyone-my dad, mom, or uncle. It doesn't reflect the uniqueness of my mom." This suggests that personalization alone is insufficient; the input must carry emotional meaning or reflect traits that participants associate with their parents to trigger a sense of closeness.

Summary Reflections and Divergent Perceptions. Participants generally agreed that increasing the involvement of parents improved the perceived authenticity and emotional value of the generated images. As P1 summarized, "The method with photos felt the closest to my mom because it involved more interesting elements. There were people and activities, so I felt connected." P3 added, "This method makes me feel like I'm communicating with my mother, while the other methods felt like empty voice messages."

However, not all participants experienced an improvement. P2 remained skeptical, stating, "None of the three methods really enhanced social connectedness for me - they all felt too AI-driven." This divergence highlights an important insight: beyond input data richness, the perceived emotional intent and contextual fit of content are essential for fostering social connectedness. Even when rich input is present, generic or non-distinctive imagery may fail to evoke resonance.

6   Discussion

Different Levels of Parents' Related Information Involvement Affect Connection Perception. Our study examined how different involvementlevels of parents in Gen AI art creation influence young adults' sense of social connectedness. We operationalized involvement through three escalating input modes: audio-only, audio with emotional prompts, and a combination of audio, prompt, and photo. The findings indicate that as parents' related information became more layered and explicit, participants were more likely to perceive the AI-generated images as emotionally resonant and relationally meaningful. Although richer inputs, particularly personal photos and emotional prompts, tended to evoke stronger emotional responses, our findings also highlight a key tension: more input does not always translate to greater connection.

Emotional Resonance Depends on Perceived Intent, Not Parents' Related Information Involvement. Interestingly, the relationship between the involvement of parents and emotional impact was not linear. One participant (P2), for instance, did not report a stronger sense of connectedness even in the highest-involvement condition. This divergence highlights a key insight: the effectiveness of involvement is not determined by the quantity or complexity of input, but by whether the contribution is perceived as intentional and emotionally resonant. A photo that lacks symbolic meaning or personal relevance may still feel generic or emotionally flat. In contrast, even minimal input, such as a carefully chosen emotional prompt, can evoke curiosity or reflection if the recipient perceives it as meaningful. Thus, it is perceived emotional intent, not the volume of contribution, that mediates the impact of human involvement on social connectedness.

Interpreting Involvement as Effort Enhances Relational Meaning. Participants often described stronger social connectedness when they believed their parents had consciously shaped the message or made a thoughtful contribution. This aligns with previous HCI findings that perceived effort and intentionality enhance emotional connection in mediated communication [18, 40]. In our study, Method 3 was particularly effective when users could attribute specific visual elements to their parents' personal context, such as daily routines, familiar places, or a visual style. Rather than the image itself, it was the interpretation of the parent's presence within it that made the experience meaningful.

Design Implications: Making Human Involvement Visible. These insights highlight key implications for future systems. Designers should move beyond simply adding more data to support users in crafting emotionally expressive inputs. For example, systems might allow parents to annotate their contributions (e.g., "This photo is from the park where we used to walk"), or offer prompts that help surface emotionally meaningful memories and associations. Importantly, AI should act as a co-creator that enhances-not masks-the user's voice, especially by supporting users who struggle with emotional expression. By amplifying their intentions and making their efforts more easily perceived by family members, AI can help ensure that even subtle attempts at connection are received with emotional clarity.

At the same time, the visual coherence and emotional plausibility of AI-generated output must be carefully considered. Participants in our study noted that when the resulting images appeared too artificial, abstract, or disconnected from everyday experience, their ability to perceive emotional intent decreased. This suggests that the effectiveness of human involvement depends not only on what is contributed but also on how that contribution is rendered by AI. The interplay between human input and AI output must therefore be designed to support both expressive depth and naturalism, so that the resulting visuals feel emotionally believable, contextually appropriate, and personally resonant.

Limitation and Future Work. This study has several limitations. To maintain experimental control, image generation followed fixed visual rules and a stylized landscape format, which reduced personalization and introduced specific visual metaphors that may not suit all users. This could limit the perceived emotional resonance. In addition, the short duration of the study prevented the observation of long-term emotional dynamics. Future work should involve extended real-world deployments and explore more adaptive and expressive visualization approaches.

7   Conclusion

By designing a system that transforms sound, emotional prompts, and photos into visual artworks, we found that more individualized inputs, particularly those containing traces of everyday life, often enhanced among adults' emotional perception and feelings of closeness. However, this effect was not always linear; its impact depended on whether the recipient could perceive the emotional intent and the expressive effort behind the input. Even when contributions were abundant, images that appeared too artificial or lacked symbolic meaning often failed to elicit emotional resonance. Therefore, system design should aim to strike an appropriate balance in the level of human involvement, with a stronger emphasis on supporting users in expressing their emotions while ensuring that AI-generated outputs remain emotionally credible and contextually appropriate. Our findings underscore the importance of positioning AI as an amplifier of emotional expression, especially for users who may struggle with articulating feelings, so that their efforts can be more easily understood and appreciated by family members. Future work should extend this approach to a wider range of family structures, longer-term deployments, and adaptive visualization mechanisms that support the sustained emotional value of human-AI co-creation in intimate relationships.

References

1. Aron, A., Aron, E.N., Smollan, D.: Inclusion of other in the self scale and the structure of interpersonal closeness. J. Pers. Soc. Psychol. **63**(4), 596–612 (1992)
2. Basole, R.C., Major, T.: Generative AI for visualization: opportunities and challenges. IEEE Comput. Graphics Appl. **44**(2), 55–64 (2024). https://doi.org/10.1109/MCG.2024.3362168
3. Baumeister, R.F., Leary, M.R.: The need to belong: desire for interpersonal attachments as a fundamental human motivation. Psychol. Bull. **117**(3), 497–529 (1995). https://doi.org/10.1037/0033-2909.117.3.497
4. Brenny, S., Hu, J.: Social connectedness and inclusion by digital augmentation in public spaces. In: 8th International Conference on Design and Semantics of Form and Movement (DeSForM 2013), Wuxi, China, pp. 108–118 (2013)
5. Consolvo, S., Roessler, P., Shelton, B.E.: The CareNet display: lessons learned from an in home evaluation of an ambient display. In: Davies, N., Mynatt, E.D., Siio, I. (eds.) UbiComp 2004. LNCS, vol. 3205, pp. 1–17. Springer, Heidelberg (2004). https://doi.org/10.1007/978-3-540-30119-6_1

6. Dalsgaard, T., Skov, M.B., Thomassen, B.R.: eKISS: sharing experiences in families through a picture blog. In: Proceedings of the 21st British HCI Group Annual Conference on People and Computers: HCI...but Not as We Know It, BCS-HCI 2007, pp. 67–75 (2007)

7. Davis, K., Owusu, E.B., Marcenaro, L., Hu, J., Regazzoni, C.S., Feijs, L.: Pervasive sensing for social connectedness. In: Enhanced Living Environments: From Models to Technologies, Series, pp. 49–79. Institution of Engineering and Technology (IET) (2017)

8. Davis, K., Owusu, E., Hu, J., Marcenaro, L., Regazzoni, C., Feijs, L.: Promoting social connectedness through human activity-based ambient displays. In: Proceedings of the International Symposium on Interactive Technology and Ageing Populations, Kochi, Japan, pp. 64–76 (2016)

9. Davis, K., et al.: Presenting a real-time activity-based bidirectional framework for improving social connectedness. In: Rojas, I., Joya, G., Catala, A. (eds.) IWANN 2017. LNCS, vol. 10306, pp. 356–367. Springer, Cham (2017). https://doi.org/10.1007/978-3-319-59147-6_31

10. Draxler, F., et al.: The AI ghostwriter effect: when users do not perceive ownership of AI-generated text but self-declare as authors. ACM Trans. Comput.-Hum. Interact. 31(2), 40 pages (2024). https://doi.org/10.1145/3637875. Article 25

11. Du, Q., Wei, X., Li, J., et al.: AI as a bridge across ages: exploring the opportunities of artificial intelligence in supporting inter-generational communication in virtual reality. arXiv preprint arXiv:2410.17909 (2024)

12. Eric, T.G., Di Caro, L., Rapp, A.: Human-AI collaboration insights from music composition. In: Generative AI and HCI Workshop Proceedings, GenAICHI 2024 (2024)

13. Fujita, H., Nishimoto, K.: Lovelet: a heartwarming communication tool for intimate people by constantly conveying situation data. In: CHI 2004 Extended Abstracts on Human Factors in Computing Systems, CHI EA 2004, vol. 1553 (2004). https://doi.org/10.1145/985921.986129

14. Gianet, E.T., Di Caro, L., Rapp, A.: Human-AI collaboration insights from music composition. In: GenAICHI: CHI 2024 Workshop on Generative AI and HCI, Honolulu, HI, USA. ACM (2024). https://iris.unito.it/retrieve/fd062785-090c-4058-8098-17427854af31/2024-CHI.pdf

15. Gozalo-Brizuela, R., Garrido Merchan, E.E.: A survey of generative AI applications. J. Comput. Sci. 20(8), 801–818 (2024). https://doi.org/10.3844/jcssp.2024.801.818

16. Grenader, E., Gasques Rodrigues, D., Nos, F., Weibel, N.: The VideoMob interactive art installation connecting strangers through inclusive digital crowds. ACM Trans. Interact. Intell. Syst. 5(2), 7 (2015). https://doi.org/10.1145/2768208

17. Haslam, C., Haslam, S.A.: Social connectedness and health. In: Pachana, N.A. (ed.) Encyclopedia of Geropsychology, pp. 1–10. Springer, Singapore (2015). https://doi.org/10.1007/978-981-287-080-3_46-2

18. Hassenzahl, M., Heidecker, S., Eckoldt, K., et al.: All you need is love: current strategies of mediating intimate relationships through technology. ACM Trans. Comput.-Hum. Interact. 19(4), 19 pages (2012). https://doi.org/10.1145/2395131.2395137. Article 30

19. Hu, J., Xue, M., Yao, C., Feng, Y., Li, J., Hansen, P.: Workshop on aesthetics of connectivity for empowerment at ACM designing interactive systems 2024. In: Workshop on Aesthetics of Connectivity for Empowerment – Considerations and Challenges, ACM Conference on Designing Interactive Systems 2024 (DIS 2024), arXiv preprint arXiv:2503.23460, Copenhagen-DK (2025)

20. Le, N., Nguyen, N.V.T., Dang, T.: Real-time sound visualization via multidimensional clustering and projections. In: Proceedings of the 12th International Conference on Advances in Information Technology IAIT 2021, vol. 35, 6 pages (2021). https://doi.org/10.1145/3468784.3471604

21. Liang, D., Thomaz, E.: Audio-based activities of daily living (ADL) recognition with large-scale acoustic embeddings from online videos. Proc. ACM Interact. Mob. Wearable Ubiquitous Technol. **3**(1), 17 (2019). https://doi.org/10.1145/3314404. 18 pages

22. Liaqat, A., Axtell, B., Munteanu, C.: "With a hint she will remember": collaborative storytelling and culture sharing between immigrant grandparents and grandchildren via magic thing designs. Proc. ACM Hum.-Comput. Interact. **6**(CSCW2), 268 (2022). https://doi.org/10.1145/3555158. 37 pages

23. Lin, X., Liu, X., Rauterberg, M., Hu, J.: Take a photo for my story: social connectedness for the elderly. In: Streitz, N., Konomi, S. (eds.) HCII 2019. LNCS, vol. 11587, pp. 390–407. Springer, Cham (2019). https://doi.org/10.1007/978-3-030-21935-2_30

24. Lu, T., Hu, J.: A-vibe: exploring the impact of animal-form avatars on students' connectedness and social presence through delivering honest signals in live online classes. In: Design and Semantics of Form and Movement (DeSForM), Hong Kong, pp. 17–29 (2023)

25. Lu, T., Hu, J.: E-motioning: exploring the effects of emotional generative visuals on creativity and connectedness during videoconferencing. In: IASDR 2023: Life-Changing Design, Italy, Milan (2023)

26. Moffat, D.C., Kelly, M.E.: Artificial intelligence creates art? An experimental investigation of the influence of AI on the evaluation and appreciation of art. J. Creat. Behav. **57**(3), 1–14 (2023). https://doi.org/10.1002/jocb.600

27. Moura, F.T., Castrucci, C., Hindley, C.: Artificial intelligence creates art? An experimental investigation of value and creativity perceptions. J. Creat. Behav. **57**(4), 534–549 (2023). https://doi.org/10.1002/jocb.600

28. Ottley, A.: Adaptive and Personalized Visualization. Springer, Cham (2020). https://doi.org/10.1007/978-3-031-02607-2

29. Ragot, M., Martin, N., Cojean, S.: AI-generated vs. human artworks. A Perception Bias Towards Artificial Intelligence? In: Extended Abstracts of the 2020 CHI Conference on Human Factors in Computing Systems, CHI EA 2020, pp. 1–10 (2020). https://doi.org/10.1145/3334480.3382892

30. Rowan, J., Mynatt, E.D.: Digital family portrait field trial: support for aging in place. In: Proceedings of the SIGCHI Conference on Human Factors in Computing Systems, CHI 2005, pp. 521–530 (2005). https://doi.org/10.1145/1054972.1055044

31. Saslis-Lagoudakis, G., Cheverst, K., Dix, A., et al.: Hermes@home: supporting awareness and intimacy between distant family members. In: Proceedings of the 18th Australia Conference on Computer-Human Interaction: Design: Activities, Artefacts and Environments, OZCHI 2006, pp. 23–30 (2006). https://doi.org/10.1145/1228175.1228183

32. Schepman, A., Rodway, P.: Initial validation of the general attitudes towards artificial intelligence scale. Comput. Hum. Behav. Rep. **1**, 100014 (2020). https://doi.org/10.1016/j.chbr.2020.100014

33. Schepman, A., Rodway, P.: The general attitudes towards artificial intelligence scale (GAAIS): confirmatory validation and associations with personality, corporate distrust, and general trust. Int. J. Hum.-Comput. Interact. **39**(13), 2724–2741 (2023). https://doi.org/10.1080/10447318.2022.2085400

34. Schnizer, K., Mayer, S.: User-centered AI for data exploration: rethinking GenAI's role in visualization. arXiv preprint arXiv:2504.04253 (2025)
35. Neustaedter, C., et al.: Sharing domestic life through long-term video connections. ACM Trans. Comput.-Hum. Interact. **22**(1), 3 (2015). https://doi.org/10.1145/2696869
36. Shin, J.Y., Rheu, M., Huh-Yoo, J., Peng, W.: Designing technologies to support parent-child relationships: a review of current findings and suggestions for future directions. Proc. ACM Hum.-Comput. Interact. **5**(CSCW2), 441 (2021). https://doi.org/10.1145/3479585
37. Simon, L., Klass, L., Lammert, A. B., Froehlich, B., Ehlers, J., Hornecker, E.: Social VR activities should support ongoing conversation - comparing older and young adults' desires and requirements. In: Proceedings of the 2024 ACM Symposium on Spatial User Interaction (SUI 2024), Article 19, 13 pages. ACM, New York (2024). https://doi.org/10.1145/3677386.3682089
38. Smith, J.A.: Hermeneutics, human sciences and health: linking theory and practice. Int. J. Qual. Stud. Health Well Being **2**(1), 3–11 (2007). https://doi.org/10.1080/17482620601016120
39. Van Bel, D.T., IJsselsteijn, W.A., de Kort, Y.A.W.: Interpersonal connectedness: conceptualization and directions for a measurement instrument. In: CHI 2008 Extended Abstracts on Human Factors in Computing Systems, pp. 3129–3134. ACM, New York (2008). https://doi.org/10.1145/1358628.1358819
40. Vetere, F., Davis, H., Gibbs, M., Howard, S.: The magic box and collage: responding to the challenge of distributed intergenerational play. Int. J. Hum Comput Stud. **67**(2), 165–178 (2009). https://doi.org/10.1016/j.ijhcs.2008.09.004
41. Wang, Q., Streithorst, L., He, C., Feijs, L., Hu, J.: Calm digital artwork for connectedness: a case study. In: International Conference on Entertainment Computing - ICEC 2023, Singapore, pp. 461–470 (2023)
42. Wang, J., Yuan, X., Hu, S., Lu, Z.: AI paintings vs. human paintings? Deciphering public interactions and perceptions towards AI-generated paintings on TikTok. arXiv preprint arXiv:2409.11911 (2024)
43. Weisz, J.D., He, J., Muller, M., Hoefer, G., Miles, R., Geyer, W.: Design principles for generative AI applications. In: Proceedings of the 2024 CHI Conference on Human Factors in Computing Systems, Honolulu, HI, USA, Article 378, pp. 1–22. ACM (2024). https://doi.org/10.1145/3613904.3642466
44. Weisz, J.D., He, J., Muller, M., et al.: Design principles for generative AI applications. In: Proceedings of the 2024 CHI Conference on Human Factors in Computing Systems, CHI 2024, vol. 378, 22 pages (2024). https://doi.org/10.1145/3613904.3642466
45. Winstone, L., Mars, B., Haworth, C.M.A., et al.: Social media use and social connectedness among adolescents in the united kingdom: a qualitative exploration of displacement and stimulation. BMC Public Health **21**, 1736 (2021). https://doi.org/10.1186/s12889-021-11802-9
46. World Health Organisation: Refugee and Migrant Health. https://www.who.int/health-topics/refugee-and-migrant-health. Accessed 2020
47. Xue, M., Yao, C., Hu, J., Hu, Y., Lyu, H.: Digital arts and health. In: Göbl, B., van der Spek, E., Baalsrud Hauge, J., McCall, R. (eds.) ICEC 2022. LNCS, vol. 13477, pp. 436–442. Springer, Cham (2022). https://doi.org/10.1007/978-3-031-20212-4_37
48. Xue, M., Yao, C., Hu, J., Hu, Y., Lyu, H., Feng, Y.: Aesthetics and empowerment: exploring AI-driven creativity. In: Entertainment Computing – ICEC 2024, Manaus, BR, pp. 316–320 (2024)

49. Yang, Y., Ryokai, K.: Exploring laughter sound visualizations for self reflection. In: Proceedings of the 2022 ACM Designing Interactive Systems Conference, pp. 1472–1485. ACM, Virtual Event, Australia (2022). https://doi.org/10.1145/3532106.3533546
50. Ye, Y., et al.: Generative AI for visualization: state of the art and future directions. arXiv preprint arXiv:2404.18144 (2024)
51. Ye, Y., Hao, J., Hou, Y., et al.: Generative AI for visualization: state of the art and future directions. Vis. Inform. **8**(2), 65–76 (2024). https://doi.org/10.1016/j.visinf.2024.01.003
52. Yoo, M., Odom, W., Berger, A., et al.: Remembering through sound: co-creating sound-based mementos together with people with blindness. In: Proceedings of the 2024 CHI Conference on Human Factors in Computing Systems, CHI 2024, vol. 886, 19 pages (2024). https://doi.org/10.1145/3613904.3641940
53. Zhang, Y., Gosline, R.: Human favoritism, not AI aversion: People's perceptions (and bias) toward generative AI, human experts, and human-GAI collaboration in persuasive content generation. Judgm. Decis. Mak. **18**, e41 (2023). https://doi.org/10.1017/jdm.2023.37
54. Zheng, X., Li, Z., Gui, X., et al.: Customizing emotional support: how do individuals construct and interact with LLM-powered chatbots. arXiv preprint arXiv:2504.12943 (2025)

Designing In-Built Mini-Games for Chatbots: Opportunity to Improve User Engagement in Customer Service and Education

A. R. M. C. D. Ratnayake[(✉)] [iD]

Ningbo Global Innovation Center, Zhejiang University, Ningbo, China
22351408@zju.edu.cn

Abstract. Chatbots are increasingly deployed across diverse sectors, offering automated customer support, personalized recommendations, and streamlined information retrieval. Recent studies have shown the potential of playful elements such as gamification to enhance engagement without compromising utility. Nevertheless, studies on leveraging the minigames in chatbots to sustain engagement and improve user experiences are still unexplored. The current study reports on initial data obtained from a survey designed to evaluate user attitudes toward incorporating context-aware mini-games into chatbot interfaces and functional prototypes developed for in-situ testing. The results point to a mostly favorable user reaction; about 66.7% of polled said context-aware mini-games would make chatbot interactions more enjoyable; 62.2% said such capabilities would make repeat use more probable. Seventeen-point-eight percent of those polled voiced concerns about possible distractions, especially in task-specific contexts. These first findings point to a possibly proper function for mini-games in chatbot design, justifying more work on prototype implementations guided by these insights.

Keywords: Chatbots · Embedded mini games · User engagement

1 Introduction

Recently, chatbots represent one of the most common implementations of artificial intelligence and have drastically changed the way organizations around the world interact with customers and users. This is very true in the field of education where chat-bots using artificial intelligence can provide a natural and personal user experience and offer fast service for learner needs and problems [1, 2]. Prior research demonstrates that educational chatbots face challenges such as low levels of engagement [3]. It has also been indicated that students generally do not engage deeply when they learn via chatbot and therefore have limited learning experiences [4]. Also, the complexity of the prompt increased task completion time [5], based on survey data, users were stalled periodically while attempting to create detailed or complex answers (Fig. 2). While customer care chatbots are functioning 24/7 and they will have ability to do number of simultaneous interactions, allowing organizations to grow revenue and strengthen relationships with

© IFIP International Federation for Information Processing 2025
Published by Springer Nature Switzerland AG 2025
R. Yamanishi et al. (Eds.): ICEC 2025 Workshops, LNCS 15935, pp. 92–105, 2025.
https://doi.org/10.1007/978-3-032-02534-0_10

customers [6]. Unfortunately, due to technological limitations, limited-function chatbots also rely on limited-service quality [7]. Rapidly attaining operational limits [8]. In more intricate situations, a shift to a human is required [9]. This may result in prolonged waiting periods due to the restricted availability of client agents. Considering humans utilize chatbots for rapid and efficient problem-solving, inadequate or poorly structured handovers negate their benefits. Consequently, handovers are a crucial element for perception [10]. Perceived attributes encompass the objectively quantifiable waiting time and the subjective waiting experience [11]. The "psychology of waiting" has a longstanding history in human-computer interaction and user experience design studies. Although this study [12], indicate that dynamic reaction delays can enhance perceptions of chatbots, other research [13] presents differing conclusions. This work [14] demonstrated that reaction delay may compromise service quality in a customer service context. Consequently, a chatbot exhibiting reaction delays rather than providing instantaneous replies was correlated with diminished likability. Rapidly shifting from a passive consuming environment to one focusing on customer involvement through immersive service delivery in chatbots, incorporating contemporary technologies and service personalization is significant [15]. Recent studies identify playful interactions as crucial in adopting conversational agents [16, 17]. This allows individuals to experiment with the system and seek personal fulfillment through social interaction. Research has examined incorporating various elements, such as humor [18] and conversational styles [19], into chatbots to improve user engagement; nevertheless, the integration of minigames remains uninvestigated. We propose the incorporation of built-in minigames, an interesting way of integrating interactive game elements directly within chatbot interfaces, which has the potential to redefine user experience, utilizing the recently examined psychological theory of consumer fun [20]alongside the more established self-determination theory [21].

As a first step toward understanding this design space, we conducted a survey (N = 45) evaluating user receptiveness to in-built mini-games in chatbot contexts. This exploratory approach aligns with established HCI methodologies for novel interaction paradigms [22, 23] Particularly when investigating emergent tension between playfulness and utility, following the best practices in chatbot research and development [24]. We prioritized attitudinal measurement before behavioral implementations, as preliminary user feedback is critical for validating unconventional design approaches [25].

We embedded mini-games in order to enhance the user experience of educational and customer service chatbots. Alternatively, this concept can be applied to entertainment-focused chatbots, enabling users to have more engaging and enjoyable interactions. Prototype chatbots have been developed using HTML, CSS, and JavaScript, featuring three distinct mini-games: a card-flipping memory game, trivia Quiz (Questions are generated based on conversation) and a simple web-based tic-tac-toe game. These prototypes are connected to an open API to facilitate general conversational capabilities, serving as a fully functional basic testing ground for the proposed chatbot enhancements.

This study identifies an area with limited prior investigation and proposes a novel approach that presents opportunities for developing more engaging and user-friendly chatbots capable of providing educational support, customer assistance or relevant other chatbots. The primary objective is to evaluate user perceptions regarding the integration of mini-games and to develop prototypes informed by user feedback.

2 Background and Related Work

Games are a fundamental part of human culture and civilization around the world. They help to generate motivation and engagement [26]. The principles of play-based games are largely being applied in non-gaming contexts, such as primary and secondary education [27], in adult and higher education [28], within the healthcare and fitness industries [29], and in consumer behavior[30]. While there are many contexts in which games and/or gaming features and aesthetics are used in order to motivate people, elicit action, create learning opportunities, and address problems/challenges [31].

2.1 The Psychological Theory of Consumer Fun

Fun is a joyful experience characterized by subjective sentiments of delight, amusement, and a light-hearted attitude [18]. The psychological basis of fun was described using a psychological theory of consumer fun. According to this idea, fun is a liberating, hedonistic activity that allows a brief escape from psychological restriction [20]. Enjoyment refers to a subjective evaluation of one's experience which is highly dependent on the individual's background. Different industries are focused on creating enjoyment to stimulate positive consumer actions. An area of focus for service providers, therefore, is creating an opportunity to experience the joy, and this is profitable for the companies [32]. This way, customers become immersed in a really enjoyable experience [33]. As it becomes important to build engagement features in chatbot design, one reason is that it adds value to new technology and encourages consumer uptake while also keeping the consumers engaged with the brand [34]. Enjoyment creates a sense of excitement, and emotions will positively enhance consumer-brand engagement [33],. Research indicates that individuals' enjoyment is influenced by the satisfaction of motivational demands in previous studies on entertainment-oriented applications, such as games [35]. Thereby, this work argues that an integrated mini-game can enhance user engagement, following the psychological theory of consumer enjoyment.

2.2 Chatbot Engagement Strategies

To date, most research on how user engage with chatbots has largely emphasized the optimization of functional aspects of interaction, particularly regarding the efficiency of conversational flow and personalization [36]. The technical avenues of intent recognition improvement and natural language generation developments [37], have been powerful in demonstrating success in shortening task completion times, yet longitudinal research (over time) shows some benefits in that respect but ongoing decay in engagement at comparative levels to human mediated interaction [38]. Further, even though methodologies to personalize interaction based on user profiling [39] and contextual adaptation [40], has some reported efficacy, these generally operate on the cognitive base of engagement related to user experience, in terms of the emotional base on which engagement is frequently contacted, usually associated with establishing a deeper connection to the chatbot or the human user experience [41]. Research has shown the value of playfulness in chatbots with positive results [18, 19]; however, little no to research exists on built-in interactive mini-games. This is a huge limitation since new research from service design and educational technology shows that emotional engagement can be just as important for long-term use [42]. The continuing focus on utilitarian design of transactional chatbots presents an important opportunity to investigate playful interaction modes. Especially, as previous research shows the ability of game-based elements and micro playful interventions to sustain intrinsic motivation in connected application fields [43]. Research has shown the value of playfulness in chatbots with positive results [18, 19].

2.3 Playful Design in HCI

Playful design has emerged as a prominent paradigm for human-computer inter-action by bridging the functional utility of technology and experiential enjoyment of users. Based on notions of intrinsic motivation, High-quality motivation, such as intrinsic motivation, is associated with greater results than low-quality motivation, such as motivation derived from extrinsic rewards [44]. The design philosophy is interested in developing better, more enjoyable experiences by allowing people to explore and play (the natural human inclination). By incorporating game-like elements of challenges, rewards, and progression systems playful interfaces help enhance user interaction and experience beyond simple notions of usability. By integrating gamified elements playful interfaces provide a more enjoyable and engaging experiences for users resulting in better results like satisfaction [45] and enjoyment [46], which leads to greater interactivity, motivation, and system satisfaction [47]. Education technology sites like Duolingo showcase how micro-games and micro-rewards can help in ensuring long-term stickiness by converting boring activities into goal-oriented affairs that enhance user interactivity, fun, and learning effectiveness. Though gamified interventions have been shown to enhance user motivation and retention, the incorporation of game-like features such as points, levels, and challenges has the potential to enhance the process of learning as more engaging and rewarding [31]. E-commerce apps show that ludic elements can fit with transactional goals by means of interactive product discovery using playful chatbots [48].

2.4 Game Elements in Conversational Agents

Game-related ideas depend on context rather than having universally applicable definitions. "Playing" refers to spontaneous and exploratory activity, whereas "gaming" indicates a more structured experience characterized by established rules and objectives [47]. The concept of gamification extends to the integration of game aspects into nongaming contexts, primarily to improve user experience and engagement [49]. Although present studies have mostly looked at playfulness in the contexts of committed gaming or gamified environments, Recently, game elements have been suggested as potential tools for learning and engagement [50, 51], and significant interest has emerged regarding customer engagement through games [52, 53]. Incorporating playful elements as a novel strategy to enhance user experience is a promising approach [54, 55]; however, this remains largely unexamined in functional systems like transactional conversational chat-bots [41, 56]. The ultimate challenge is the application of existing understanding to the specifics of chatbots with mini games. This tension, while not thoroughly examined in the current literature, is the focus of this work. Intentionally incorporating playful design elements into chatbot conversations to explore the user experience, without detracting from the chatting condition's essential ability to perform the tasks to which it is assigned. The design of a useful chatbot system is an important but complicated component of achieving this balance between spontaneity and task orienting. Thus, further academic research is necessary to clarify our understanding of how to best achieve this balance.

3 Methodology

This paper looks at the inclusion of interactive mini-games into transactional chatbot experiences using a research-through-design method. This work lays the groundwork for context-aware, playful design in conversational interfaces by combining empirical user insights from an exploratory survey phase and iterative prototyping. This paper used a two-phase methodological approach: (1) an initial exploratory survey phase, followed by (2) a prototype development phase guided by the insights collected from the survey.

3.1 Survey Goals, Participation and Structure

The survey was designed to address four key research objectives: identifying common user frustrations in current chatbot interactions, with a particular focus on wait times and repetitive task fatigue; evaluating user receptiveness to mini-games as a novel engage-ment strategy; determining optimal game characteristics, including preferred types, dura-tions, and conditions; and assessing privacy concerns specific to game-integrated chat-bot interactions. These research goals were established to bridge the knowledge gap between traditional usability-focused chatbot research and emerging playful interaction paradigms.

For our investigation, we engaged with a diverse group of young adults from Sri Lanka through online communities, including university students, vocational trainees, and early-career professionals. We sought individuals who actively utilize online plat-forms and applications for educational, professional, and social networking, ensuring a sample familiar with digital communication tools. The final sample comprised 45 par-ticipants, with careful attention paid to balancing representation from both educational (n = 25) and customer service chatbot users (n = 20). This stratification enabled a comparative analysis of these two key use cases. Recruitment materials highlighted the study's objective of enhancing chatbot experiences, while intentionally omitting specific hypotheses regarding mini-games to prevent priming effects and maintain the integrity of participant responses.

The survey instrument was composed of 25 meticulously crafted questions, care-fully organized into four thematic sections to ensure comprehensive data collection. The first section was dedicated to gathering essential demographic information from partic-ipants, including their age, gender identity, and educational background. This section also served as a screening mechanism to identify participants with relevant experience in interacting with chatbots, ensuring that the subsequent data collected would be informed by genuine user experiences. The second section delved into the exploration of usage patterns, employing questions specifically designed to capture details regarding the frequency of interactions, the duration of each session, and the specific challenges or pain points that user encountered during their chatbot interactions. This aimed to provide a nuanced understanding of how users engage with chatbots in practice. The third section was exclusively focused on investigating user preferences related to mini-games within chatbot environments. It utilized Likert-scale items as a means to assess participants' attitudes toward a diverse range of game types and scenarios, allowing for a quantitative assessment of user inclinations. The final section was designed to address user data privacy, aiming to understand users' concerns and perceptions regarding the handling of their personal information by chatbots. Quantitative data obtained from the survey was subjected to analysis using descriptive statistics. This analytical approach aimed to reveal general trends and patterns in user behavior and preferences, providing valuable insights into how individuals interact with chatbots and their attitude towards the mini game built chatbots.

3.2 Developed Prototypes

Three web-based chatbot prototypes were developed using HTML5, CSS3, and JavaScript, integrated with OpenAI's API for natural language processing (see Fig. 1) Our design concept involved progressively developing three interactive chatbot prototypes using standard web technologies HTML, CSS, and JavaScript with OpenAI's GPT-3.5 Turbo API powering the core conversation. The initial prototype focused on dynamic learning by generating quizzes. It tracked the last three chat exchanges and, when the user typed 'let's play,' used this immediate context to prompt OpenAI for three multiple-choice questions (received as JSON), which JavaScript then displayed in the chat. We then improved the user interface using the second prototype by adding a modal pop-up for a 4x4 memory game. This highlighted a different engagement approach triggered by a comparable 'let's play' cue; JavaScript managed all game logic from card shuffling and CSS-driven flip animations to state control. The most advanced prototype simulated a customer service environment. JavaScript generated interactive FAQ buttons within the chat. If a user chose to 'Contact Agent,' a simulated two-minute wait began, during which they could play an embedded Tic-Tac-Toe game (again, a JavaScript-driven modal). A key feature here was AI persona adaptation: after the wait, a new API call, providing the chat history and instructing OpenAI to respond as a human agent, initiated the 'agent's' reply and simultaneously triggered JavaScript to automatically close the game modal. This demonstrated dynamic content switching and state-aware UI updates. Across all versions, asynchronous fetch calls ensured responsive communication with the OpenAI service.

4   Results and Discussion

Quantitative data from the survey was analyzed using descriptive statistics, whereby focusing on two important survey questions relative to waiting time (Q8), boredom (Q10), feelings, during the waiting time or boredom (Q13), interest in chatbot with

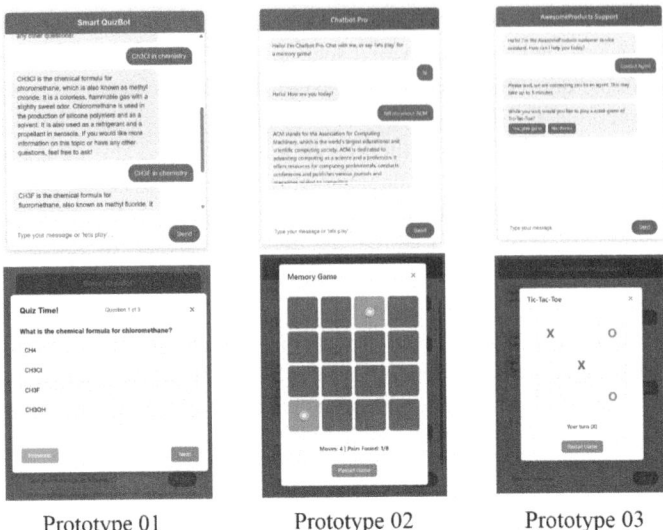

| Prototype 01 | Prototype 02 | Prototype 03 |

Fig. 1. Developed Fully functional Games in built chatbot prototypes.

mini-games (Q21), and projected feelings of positivity for using game mini with the chatbot (Q22), and reported in Table 1. The subsequent sections report the results from the data analysis in the same structured format as the questionnaire, with key feedback summarized and presented in a visual format.

Table 1. Perceptions of Waiting, Boredom, and Game-Based Engagement in Chatbot Use.

Question	Mean	SD	Mode
Q8	3.60	0.93	4
Q10	3.22	1.03	3
Q13	3.64	1.09	4
Q21	3.98	0.84	4
Q22	3.89	0.81	4

4.1 Section 01 – Negative User Experiences with Traditional Conversational AI

Examining survey data from questions Q7 to Q13 uncovered insights on users' present negative experiences with conversational artificial intelligence. The analysis of user-reported waiting times in chatbot interactions (Q7) reveals that delays are most commonly experienced with customer support chatbots (52.4%), followed by Educational or learning chatbots (42.9%), and Shopping assistance chatbots (21.4%), the overall frequency of waiting times (Q8) reported experiencing moderate to frequent waiting times. The descriptive statistics for this item (M = 3.60, SD = 0.93, Mode = 4) support the assertion that frequent waiting is a prevalent issue, reflecting moderate agreement among respondents. User behaviors with the waiting times were the focus of (Q9), which demonstrated Majority of users (34.1%) tend to switch to another task or APP, followed by patiently wait until chatbot reply (29.3%). Data analysis of (Q11) points out that boredom was experienced by Majority of educational chatbot users (62.2%) yet not all the respondents respond to this question, followed by customer care chatbots (30%), and in (Q10) overall frequency of descriptive statistics (M = 3.22, SD = 1.03, Mode = 3) Supports towards occasional boredom. However, responses vary more with the low number of responses. Q12 Focused on user behaviors during bored times, the Majority responded positively toward switching to another task (27.5%), followed by playing games or checking social media (25%). In (Q13), users express their emotions in wait-ing times and mentally fatigued or bored times, indicating the Majority being annoyed (44.4%), followed by frustrations (20%). Supported by descriptive statistics, negative emotions are common, but responses are diverse. (M = 3.64, SD = 1.09 Mode = 4). (see Fig. 2).

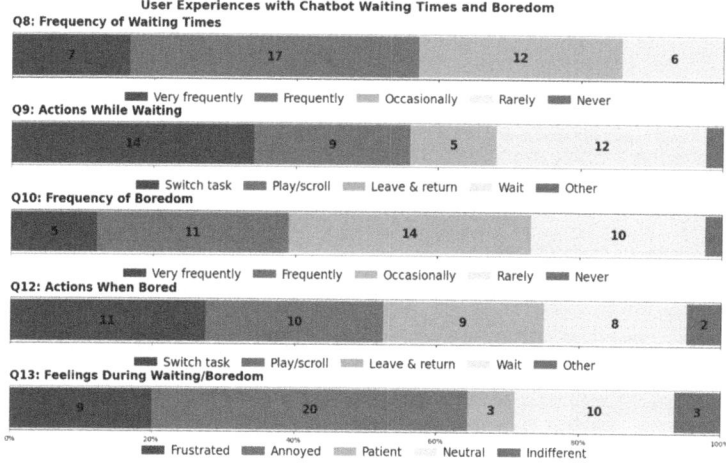

Fig. 2. Participants attitude towards traditional chatbots.

4.2 Section 02 – Possible Opportunities with Mini-Games as an Intervention

This section assesses users' views about using integrated mini-games in chatbots. In (Q14) users were questioned about prior experience with inbuilt games to chatbots; 91.1% of respondents indicated that they have no prior experience with these types of systems, while a small 8.9% of the respondents indicated that they have had something of a previous experience. The next (Q15) was about users' perception towards playing a mini-game built into a chatbot; the majority (66.7%) of respondents had a positive prospect towards playing mini-games in a chatbot, while 15.6% said they would think about it, and 17.8% said they were not interested in mini-games in a chatbot. When questioning the user's idea about engagement time with a chatbot that has an inbuilt chatbot in (Q20), A total of 62.2% of users thought a mini-game could improve the amount of time that they spent with the chatbot; 20% were unsure; and 17.8% disagreed. In (Q21) users were asked about returning to a chatbot with an inbuilt mini game compared to one that does not; interpretation appears to be a positive attitude toward games; 68.2% of users said they would be at least somewhat more likely to return (31.8% much more likely, 36.4% somewhat more likely). 29.5% said there would not be a difference in likelihood, and 2.3% said they would be less likely. Supported by descriptive statistics (M = 3.98, SD = 0.84, Mode = 4) in favor of a Positive likelihood of returning to a chatbot with games. In (Q22), users mentioned their positive anticipation towards increasing the satisfaction of engaging with the game inbuild chatbot. The majority of users (47.7%) anticipated games would slightly increase satisfaction, followed by no effect on satisfaction (25%) and significantly increase being the close third (22.7%). Supported by descriptive statistics (M = 3.89, SD = 0.81, Mode = 4) showing the Positive effect of games on satisfaction. (see Fig. 3).

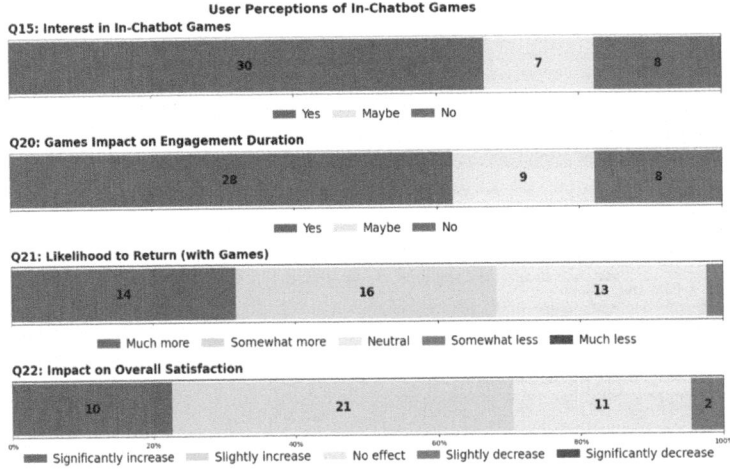

Fig. 3. Participants attitude towards inbuilt games in chatbots.

4.3 Section 3 - Design Considerations for In-Chatbot Games

User insights were used to draft the prototypes and examine the options for introducing mini-games into a chatbot. From these insights (Q16), the top three game types users liked most were memory games (58.5%), trivia quizzes (51.2%), and quick arcade games (39%). They also indicated the desired length of games (Q17). Though most users (57.1%) liked game lengths of 1–3 min, a notable minority (28.6%) deemed 3–5 min acceptable. Another significant factor was the user's expectations regarding the game's relevance to the chatbot's goal (Q18). A high proportion of users (47.6%) wanted games directly related to what the chatbot was supposed to do (the chatbot's primary purpose).

In comparison, 31.1% did not specifically say they wanted a related game, and 22.2% thought irrelevant games were acceptable. According to the (Q19) major three types of which users like to play games were entertainment chatbots (69%), followed by education (57.1%), and customer service chatbots (40.7%). The findings indicate potential uses of mini-games in various contexts. The findings from the survey also showed the importance of games being easy to learn and play upon accessing (Q23). From the data, 22.2% felt it was essential, 35.6% said it was important, 33.3% said neutral, and 8.9% said it was not very important (see Fig. 4).

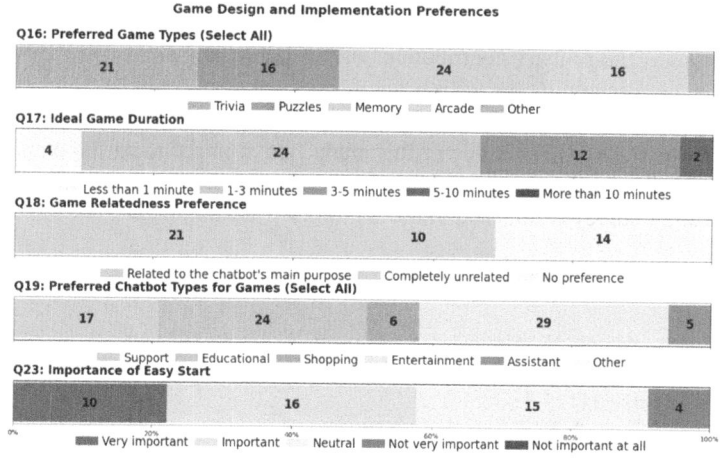

Fig. 4. Participants preferences on in built mini games.

5   Limitations and Future Work

This work is the first exploratory step toward investigating chatbot interactions using mini-games. Several important constraints must be acknowledged to help interpret the results and guide the following investigations. First, the study included a small sample and a homogeneous set of participants from one county. Second, although the prototypes demonstrated full technical functionality, prototypes are still early proofs of concept. They were to demonstrate feasibility and responses to user-informed design. Third, this phase does not include post-prototype user interviews and usability testing, which will form a barrier to implementing the concept in real-world applications. As for future work, further steps with participant diversity and the increased number of participants in the study can strengthen the generalizability of the results. Collecting qualitative data with focus groups or user interviews is another good way to learn more about how users feel about the mini-game chatbot experiences. The above can be combined with systematic usability testing with methods such as the System Usability Scale (SUS) to understand the prototype usability, which is an improvement in both the conceptual underpinnings of future work and practical adaptation to a real-world sense [57].

6 Conclusion

As more and more chatbots are deployed to the internet, new paradigms need to be explored to keep users engaged and enhance the user experience [15]. Our study represents a novel study area by implementing mini-games into chatbots. The exploratory nature of this investigation and the conclusions we developed based on simple prototypes can act as a platform for subsequent investigations. The study aimed to test user perceptions about mini-games and develop prototypes informed by users' responses. This research represents an initial foray into a relatively uncharted domain. Although survey results substantiated the conceptual background, the prototypes developed can be employed as fundamental instruments for assessing ideation with practical applications. In essence, the primary contributions of this paper encompass the exploration of the research gap concerning the utilization of mini-games in chatbots, validation of the conceptual underpinnings through survey data, and the creation of functional prototypes for further investigation. The value of this study lies in introducing the empirical and technical basis for context-aware, playful design in transactional chatbots, especially with the Phase 1 survey results and Phase 2 prototype development.

References

1. Kuhail, M.A., Alturki, N., Alramlawi, S., Alhejori, K.: Interacting with educational chatbots: a systematic review. Educ. Inf. Technol. (Dordr) **28**(1), 973–1018 (2023). https://doi.org/10.1007/s10639-022-11177-3
2. Nirala, K.K., Singh, N.K., Purani, V.S.: A survey on providing customer and public administration based services using AI: chatbot. Multimed Tools Appl. **81**(16), 22215–22246 (2022). https://doi.org/10.1007/s11042-021-11458-y
3. Atmosukarto, I., Sin, C.W., Iyer, P., Tong, N.H., Peng Yu, K.W.: Enhancing adaptive online chemistry course with AI-Chatbot. In: TALE 2021 - IEEE International Conference on Engineering, Technology and Education, Proceedings, Institute of Electrical and Electronics Engineers Inc., pp. 838–843 (2021). https://doi.org/10.1109/TALE52509.2021.9678528
4. Lin, M.P.C., Chang, D.H., Winne, P.H.: A proposed methodology for investigating student-chatbot interaction patterns in giving peer feedback. Educ. Technol. Res. Dev. (2024). https://doi.org/10.1007/s11423-024-10408-3
5. Guo, J., Tao, D., Yang, C.: The effects of continuous conversation and task complexity on usability of an AI-based conversational agent in smart home environments. In: Lecture Notes in Electrical Engineering, Springer Verlag, pp. 695–703 (2020). https://doi.org/10.1007/978-981-13-8779-1_79
6. Turban, E., Outland, J., King, D., Lee, J.K., Liang, T.-P., Turban, D.C.: Springer texts in business and economics electronic commerce 2018 a managerial and social networks perspective Ninth Edition (2018). http://www.springer.com/series/10099
7. Gnewuch, U., Morana, S., Maedche, A.: Towards designing cooperative and social conversational agents for customer service (2017). http://ksri.kit.edu
8. Mctear, M., Callejas, Z., Griol, D.: The conversational interface talking to smart devices
9. Bodrunova, S.S. (ed.), Internet Science, vol. 11193. In: Lecture Notes in Computer Science, vol. 11193. Springer, Cham (2018). https://doi.org/10.1007/978-3-030-01437-7
10. Elmorshidy, A.: Benefits analysis of live customer support chat in e-commerce websites: dimensions of a new success model for live customer support chat. In: Proceedings - 10th International Conference on Machine Learning and Applications, ICMLA 2011, pp. 325–329 (2011). https://doi.org/10.1109/ICMLA.2011.167

11. Maister, D.H.: The psychology of waiting lines (2005). www.davidmaister.com
12. Moon, Y.: The effects of physical distance and response latency on persuasion in computer-mediated communication and human-computer communication (1999)
13. Gnewuch, U., Morana, S., Adam, M.T.P., Maedche, A.: Opposing effects of response time in human-Chatbot interaction: the moderating role of prior experience. Bus. Inf. Syst. Eng. **64**(6), 773–791 (2022). https://doi.org/10.1007/s12599-022-00755-x
14. Lo, C.-W., Wang, Y.-L.: The effects of response time on older and young adults' Interaction experience with Chatbot, 19 February 2024. https://doi.org/10.21203/rs.3.rs-3960036/v1
15. Hollebeek, L.D., Menidjel, C., Sarstedt, M., Jansson, J., Urbonavicius, S.: Engaging Consumers through Artificially Intelligent Technologies: Systematic Review, Conceptual Model, and Further Research. John Wiley and Sons Inc., 01 April 2024, https://doi.org/10.1002/mar.21957
16. Luger, E., Sellen, A.: Like having a really bad pa: the gulf between user expectation and experience of conversational agents. In: Conference on Human Factors in Computing Systems - Proceedings, Association for Computing Machinery, pp. 5286–5297, May 2016. https://doi.org/10.1145/2858036.2858288
17. Ogan, A., Finkelstein, S., Mayfield, E., D'Adamo, C., Matsuda, N., Cassell, J.: 'Oh, dear Stacy!' social interaction, elaboration, and learning with teachable agents. In: Conference on Human Factors in Computing Systems - Proceedings, pp. 39–48 (2012). https://doi.org/10.1145/2207676.2207684
18. Xie, Y., Liang, C., Zhou, P., Jiang, L.: Exploring the influence mechanism of chatbot-expressed humor on service satisfaction in online customer service. J. Retail. Consum. Serv. **76** (2024). https://doi.org/10.1016/j.jretconser.2023.103599
19. Roy Bhattacharjee, D., Kuanr, A., Pradhan, D., Moharana, T.R.: Fun or warm: how conversational style boosts customer engagement. J. Retail. Consum. Serv. **85** (2025). https://doi.org/10.1016/j.jretconser.2025.104293
20. Oh, T.T., Pham, M.T.: A liberating-engagement theory of consumer fun. J. Consum. Res. **49**(1), 46–73 (2022). https://doi.org/10.1093/jcr/ucab051
21. Ryan, R.M., Deci, E.L.: Self-Determination Theory and the Facilitation of Intrinsic Motivation, Social Development, and Well-Being Self-Determination Theory, Ryan (1985)
22. Beth, M.: Rosson. In: Proceedings of the SIGCHI Conference on Human Factors in Computing Systems, ACM (2007)
23. Sengers, P., Boehner, K., David, S., Kaye, J.J.: Reflective design (2005)
24. Følstad, A., Brandtzaeg, P.B.: Chatbots and the new world of HCI. Interactions **24**(4), 38–42 (2017). https://doi.org/10.1145/3085558
25. Araujo, T.: Living up to the chatbot hype: the influence of anthropomorphic design cues and communicative agency framing on conversational agent and company perceptions. Comput Human Behav **85**, 183–189 (2018). https://doi.org/10.1016/j.chb.2018.03.051
26. Bozkurt, A., Durak, G.: A systematic review of gamification research: in pursuit of homo ludens. Int. J. Game-Based Learn. **8**(3), 15–33 (2018). https://doi.org/10.4018/IJGBL.2018070102
27. Rachels, J.R., Rockinson-Szapkiw, A.J.: The effects of a mobile gamification app on elementary students' Spanish achievement and self-efficacy. Comput. Assist. Lang. Learn. **31**(1–2), 72–89 (2018). https://doi.org/10.1080/09588221.2017.1382536
28. Huang, B., Hew, K.F., Lo, C.K.: Investigating the effects of gamification-enhanced flipped learning on undergraduate students' behavioral and cognitive engagement. Interact. Learn. Environ. **27**(8), 1106–1126 (2019). https://doi.org/10.1080/10494820.2018.1495653
29. Orji, R., Moffatt, K.: Persuasive technology for health and wellness: state-of-the-art and emerging trends. Health Inf. J. **24**(1), 66–91 (2018). https://doi.org/10.1177/1460458216650979

30. Tobon, S., Ruiz-Alba, J.L., García-Madariaga, J.: Gamification and online consumer decisions: is the game over? Decis Support Syst. **128** (2020). https://doi.org/10.1016/j.dss.2019.113167

31. Zainuddin, Z., Chu, S.K.W., Shujahat, M., Perera, C.J.: The impact of gamification on learning and instruction: a systematic review of empirical evidence. Educ. Res. Rev. **30** (2020). https://doi.org/10.1016/j.edurev.2020.100326

32. Kol, O., Lissitsa, S.: Looking for accommodations? What motivates consumer information search behavior on Instagram, Facebook groups and personal profiles on social networking sites. Inf. Technol. People **37**(4), 1696–1716 (2024). https://doi.org/10.1108/ITP-05-2022-0389

33. Prentice, C., Nguyen, M.: Engaging and retaining customers with AI and employee service. J. Retail. Consum. Serv. **56** (2020). https://doi.org/10.1016/j.jretconser.2020.102186

34. Pillai, R., Sivathanu, B., Metri, B., Kaushik, N.: Students' adoption of AI-based teacher-bots (T-bots) for learning in higher education. Inf. Technol. People **37**(1), 328–355 (2024). https://doi.org/10.1108/ITP-02-2021-0152

35. Ryan, R.M., Rigby, C.S., Przybylski, A.: The motivational pull of video games: a self-determination theory approach. Motiv. Emot. **30**(4), 347–363 (2006). https://doi.org/10.1007/s11031-006-9051-8

36. Fadhil, A., Schiavo, G.: Designing for health Chatbots, CoRR, February (2019). https://doi.org/10.48550/arXiv.1902.09022

37. Wiboolyasarin, W., Wiboolyasarin, K., Tiranant, P., Boonyakitanont, P., Jinowat, N.: Designing chatbots in language classrooms: an empirical investigation from user learning experience. Smart Learn. Environ. **11**(1) (2024). https://doi.org/10.1186/s40561-024-00319-4

38. Silva, G.R.S., Canedo, E.D.: Towards user-centric guidelines for Chatbot conversational design. Int. J. Hum. Comput. Interact. **40**(2), 98–120 (2024). https://doi.org/10.1080/10447318.2022.2118244

39. Kocaballi, A.B., et al.: The Personalization of Conversational Agents in Health Care: Systematic Review. JMIR Publications Inc., 01 November 2019. https://doi.org/10.2196/15360

40. Izadi, S., Forouzanfar, M.: Error Correction and Adaptation in Conversational AI: A Review of Techniques and Applications in Chatbots, Multidisciplinary Digital Publishing Institute (MDPI), 01 June 2024, https://doi.org/10.3390/ai5020041

41. Diederich, S., Brendel, A.B., Morana, S., Kolbe, L.: On the design of and interaction with conversational agents: an organizing and assessing review of human-computer interaction research. J. Assoc. Inf. Syst. **23**(1), 96–138 (2022). https://doi.org/10.17705/1jais.00724

42. Wollny, S., Schneider, J., Di Mitri, D., Weidlich, J., Rittberger, M., Drachsler, H.: Are We There Yet? - A Systematic Literature Review on Chatbots in Education, Frontiers Media S.A., 15 July 2021, https://doi.org/10.3389/frai.2021.654924

43. Hamari, J., Koivisto, J., Sarsa, H.: Does Gamification Work?-A Literature Review of Empirical Studies on Gamification (2014)

44. Ryan, R.M., Deci, E.L.: Intrinsic and extrinsic motivation from a self-determination theory perspective: definitions, theory, practices, and future directions. Contemp. Educ. Psychol. **61** (2020). https://doi.org/10.1016/j.cedpsych.2020.101860

45. Vlachopoulos, D., Makri, A.: The effect of games and simulations on higher education: a systematic literature review, Springer Netherlands, 01 December 2017, https://doi.org/10.1186/s41239-017-0062-1

46. Jalil, H.A., et al.: Systematic review of enjoyment element in health-related game-based learning. Int. J. Emerg. Technol. Learn. **15**(21), 40–57 (2020). https://doi.org/10.3991/ijet.v15i21.17345

47. Deterding, S., Dixon, D., Khaled, R., Nacke, L.: From game design elements to gamefulness: defining 'gamification. In: Proceedings of the 15th International Academic MindTrek Conference: Envisioning Future Media Environments, MindTrek 2011, pp. 9–15 (2011). https://doi.org/10.1145/2181037.2181040

48. "Sephora Bot — ChatbotGuide.org." Accessed 08 May 2025. https://www.chatbotguide.org/sephora-bot

49. Deterding, S., O'Hara, K., Sicart, M., Dixon, D., Nacke, L.: Gamification: using game design elements in non-gaming contexts. In: Conference on Human Factors in Computing Systems - Proceedings, pp. 2425–2428. ACM (2011). https://doi.org/10.1145/1979742.1979575

50. Barab, S., Thomas, M., Dodge, T., Carteaux, R., Tuzun, H.: Making learning fun: quest Atlantis, a game without guns

51. Rieber, L.P.: Seriously considering play: designing interactive learning environments based on the blending of microworlds, Simulations, and Games

52. (Grace) Park, H.E.: Designing engagement: Exploring affordances in freemium digital games. Technol. Soc. **81** (2025). https://doi.org/10.1016/j.techsoc.2025.102840

53. Hollebeek, L.D., Das, K., Shukla, Y.: Game on! How gamified loyalty programs boost customer engagement value. Int. J. Inf. Manage. **61** (2021). https://doi.org/10.1016/j.ijinfomgt.2021.102308

54. Benner, D., Schöbel, S., Janson, A., Leimeister, J.M.: Engaging Minds – How Gamified Chatbots Can Support and Motivate Learners in Digital Education (2024). https://doi.org/10.24251/HICSS.2024.008

55. Hamari, J., Koivisto, J.: Social motivations to use gamification: an empirical study of gamifying exercise

56. Katchapakirin, K., Anutariya, C., Supnithi, T.: ScratchThAI: a conversation-based learning support framework for computational thinking development. Educ. Inf. Technol. (Dordr) **27**(6), 8533–8560 (2022). https://doi.org/10.1007/s10639-021-10870-z

57. Beyond Human Computer Interaction4 th ED

The Ethical Reconstruction of Generative AI: Social Value, Governance Challenges, and Pathways to Digital Empowerment

Jie Tu[(✉)] [iD] and Mengjie Tang [iD]

Department of Digital Media Art, Hunan International Economics University, Changsha 410205, Hunan, China

tujie1@csu.edu.cn

Abstract. The rapid advancement of generative artificial intelligence (AI) has brought not only new possibilities for creativity, automation, and cross-domain collaboration, but also profound ethical challenges. This paper proposes a structured ethical reconstruction framework that addresses the systemic tensions emerging from the widespread integration of Generative AI into public knowledge, institutional judgment, and individual agency. First, we construct a three-dimensional model of ethical tensions across cognition, behavior, and governance, revealing how misalignment among these domains can amplify risks such as misinformation, algorithmic bias, and responsibility vacuums. Second, drawing on the theory of embedded governance, we present a multi-layered responsibility framework that integrates national regulation, platform mechanisms, organizational ethics, and user accountability. Finally, the paper affirms the irreplaceable value of human expression and judgment through three institutional mechanisms: the right to interrupt, the right to contest output, and the right to human oversight. These mechanisms are embedded into Generative AI systems via interface design, content labeling, and regulatory instruments. By combining philosophical reflection with implementable governance pathways, this study contributes to the evolving discourse on trustworthy and inclusive Generative AI, with practical implications for policy, platform design, and user ethics.

Keywords: Generative AI · AI ethics · Embedded governance

1 Introduction

Generative Artificial Intelligence (Generative AI) is rapidly reshaping how humans produce, interpret, and interact with information. From large language models like GPT-4 to multimodal systems such as DALL·E and Midjourney, these technologies have been integrated into diverse sectors including education, research, culture, justice, and industrial design [1, 2]. Their capacity to synthesize text, images, code, and semantics is transforming the foundation of knowledge creation, shifting from labor-intensive to model-driven paradigms [3].

© IFIP International Federation for Information Processing 2025
Published by Springer Nature Switzerland AG 2025
R. Yamanishi et al. (Eds.): ICEC 2025 Workshops, LNCS 15935, pp. 106–119, 2025.
https://doi.org/10.1007/978-3-032-02534-0_11

Yet this transformation introduces complex ethical challenges. A central concern is hallucination: Generative AI often fabricates coherent but factually inaccurate content, undermining the reliability of public discourse and professional judgment [4]. Simultaneously, the presence of systemic bias in training data produces outputs that perpetuate gender, racial, and cultural stereotypes, raising critical concerns about fairness and inclusion [5, 6]. Responsibility attribution remains opaque. Prompt-based interactions are largely unregulated, and developers often avoid liability by exploiting legal loopholes, weakening governance structures [7, 8].

Beyond these technical and legal issues, Generative AI challenges deeper philosophical assumptions about human agency and epistemic authority. As these systems increasingly participate in decision-making and knowledge creation, human capacity for autonomous judgment, expressive freedom, and epistemic sovereignty faces structural erosion [9, 10]. Scholars have begun to emphasize the importance of safeguarding expressive agency, calling for ethical frameworks that affirm the primacy of human judgment in AI-mediated environments [11].

Initial governance responses have emerged globally. The European Union has introduced a tiered, risk-based regulatory model emphasizing transparency and accountability [8]. The U.S. National Institute of Standards and Technology (NIST) has proposed a life-cycle-based AI Risk Management Framework [10]. UNESCO has issued global guidance promoting human-centeredness, fairness, and trustworthiness [9]. However, these approaches remain fragmented and reactive.

Three key limitations persist in the academic discourse. First, existing research is siloed—most studies isolate technical or policy issues without integrating cognitive, behavioral, and governance dimensions [12]. Second, prompt engineering by users is under-conceptualized, despite its direct impact on AI outputs [7]. Third, although the importance of human agency is widely acknowledged, few institutional mechanisms exist to operationalize rights to expression and judgment [13–15].

To address these challenges, this study raises three core questions: (1) How can we model the ethical tensions of Generative AI through a triadic framework encompassing cognition, behavior, and governance? (2) How can we design a multi-layered responsibility structure involving regulators, platforms, organizations, and users? (3) How can we affirm expressive and judgmental agency through normative and design-based interventions?

In response, this paper makes three contributions. First, it proposes the Cognition–Behavior–Governance (CBG) model to trace the structural interactions that generate ethical risk. Second, it introduces a layered governance framework embedding ethical accountability across design, deployment, and regulation stages. Third, it articulates a normative foundation to reaffirm human sovereignty in expression and judgment, proposing mechanisms that ensure AI advancement aligns with human dignity and social well-being.

Drawing on philosophical, legal, and interface-level research, this study advocates for digital empowerment—defined as the restoration of user agency, moral judgment, and institutional voice in algorithmically mediated environments shaped by Generative AI.

2 Related Work

2.1 Policy, Platforms, and Governance Challenges

The rise of Generative AI has intensified a complex entanglement of policy gaps, platform responsibilities, and legal ambiguity. A central concern is the proliferation of misinformation stemming from model hallucinations. Marcus warns that models like GPT-4 frequently produce fabricated or unverified content, threatening public knowledge reliability and decision-making integrity [16]. Tamkin et al. further show that large language models often "fill in" knowledge gaps with plausible but inaccurate data, particularly in high-stakes domains such as healthcare and education [17].

Algorithmic bias remains another persistent ethical hazard. Birhane et al. reveal that multimodal datasets embed harmful stereotypes, which manifest in biased outputs [18]. Raji et al. respond with a comprehensive auditing pipeline to uncover and mitigate these harms in large-scale AI systems [19]. Shin advances the debate by introducing "algorithmic inoculation"—a model advocating real-time prompts and cognitive scaffolds to enhance user resistance against AI-driven misinformation, thus embedding ethical interventions at the interface level [20].

Platforms play a crucial mediating role, yet most lack upstream mechanisms for prompt traceability or behavioral alignment. Instead, responsibility is deferred to post-hoc moderation, which fails to address the origin of ethical risk at the prompt–generation junction. Shin's model urges platforms to adopt interface-level affordances—such as risk-aware feedback loops and generation path visualizations—to act as proactive agents of governance [20]. Without such designs, platforms risk reinforcing disengagement and enabling misuse.

Legal frameworks have also lagged. Samuelson highlights that current copyright laws do not adequately address works generated partially or entirely by machines, leading to confusion over authorship and ownership [21]. Menell and Lemley propose hybrid reforms that combine attribution rules with AI-specific licensing models [22].

The attribution of responsibility remains especially opaque. Chesterman et al. argue that legal doctrines premised on identifiable agents are incompatible with generative AI's distributed authorship [23]. Abbott and Bogenschneider caution against shifting liability entirely to users through disclaimers, which erodes institutional accountability [24].

In sum, governance challenges in Generative AI extend beyond technical issues to include platform architecture and legal infrastructure. Addressing these requires integrated frameworks that align policy, interface design, and normative responsibility across the entire AI lifecycle.

2.2 Ethical Frameworks and Design Paradigms

Recent scholarship has increasingly highlighted the ethical challenges posed by human–AI interaction, especially with regard to diminishing user agency and normative alignment. Binns et al. report that users often overestimate the authority of AI outputs and fail to critically interrogate content, thereby eroding moral judgment and independent responsibility [25]. In education and research contexts, this pattern can accelerate a loss of critical thinking and epistemic engagement, threatening long-term innovation and integrity [26].

Philosophical accounts have contextualized these behavioral shifts within broader concerns over human subjectivity and ethical authorship. Floridi argues that the linguistic fluency of generative systems dissolves boundaries between human and machine authorship, thereby destabilizing the normative basis of originality and authorship [27]. Danaher describes a parallel process of "expressive outsourcing," wherein creative and judgmental functions are gradually delegated to algorithms, leading users to disengage from self-authorship and ethical evaluation [28].

Rather than viewing these shifts merely as cultural or psychological trends, Coeckelbergh reframes them as structural transformations in moral agency. His "paradox of machine expressivity" illustrates how increased output fluency can reduce the space for ethical choice-making and narrative autonomy [29]. These perspectives converge on a shared concern: that Generative AI systems, by design or affordance, risk marginalizing the human voice within epistemic and creative processes.

Existing ethical paradigms such as Value-Sensitive Design (VSD) and design justice have laid important theoretical foundations for embedding human values in technological systems. These models emphasize stakeholder inclusion and participatory design, and have informed a wide range of human-centered AI frameworks [29, 30]. However, with the rise of dynamic, Generative AI systems, these paradigms are being critically re-examined. Section 2.3 further explores their limitations and how this study builds upon and extends them toward an embedded governance approach.

2.3 Summary and Research Gap

While the ethical risks of Generative AI have attracted growing attention, current research reveals several unresolved limitations that impede the development of effective governance systems. This section outlines four key gaps that motivate this study's embedded governance framework.

First, existing literature remains fragmented. Technical studies address hallucination, bias, or intellectual property in isolation, without a unified framework linking prompt behavior, system affordances, and output accountability [16, 18, 21, 25]. As a result, ethical issues are diagnosed symptomatically rather than structurally.

Second, although philosophical and policy debates rightly emphasize the importance of protecting human agency, few studies propose concrete mechanisms to institutionalize rights to judgment, authorship, or expressive freedom in generative environments [27, 28]. The lack of operational safeguards leaves users vulnerable to cognitive automation, behavioral drift, and diminished ethical awareness.

Third, responsibility attribution remains underdeveloped. Legal theorists acknowledge the opacity of co-authored AI content [23, 24], yet little work has translated these insights into design-level accountability tools. Even widely adopted ethical design paradigms—such as Value-Sensitive Design (VSD)—fall short in generative contexts. VSD emphasizes participatory design and stakeholder inclusion [29, 30], but assumes static roles and bounded systems. In contrast, Generative AI features emergent content, distributed agency, and evolving misuse patterns. Recent critiques argue that VSD lacks runtime instruments for traceability, contestability, and behavioral responsiveness [31–33].

Fourth, existing scholarship remains overly focused on large language models. Multimodal generators—producing images, code, or audio—pose unique challenges of interpretability and provenance that remain poorly addressed in current governance frameworks [5, 18].

In response, this study proposes a multi-layered governance model grounded in embedded ethics. By integrating insights from legal theory, human-AI interaction, and design philosophy, it advances concrete mechanisms for layered accountability and real-time ethical alignment. The framework addresses not only what values matter, but how they can be embedded across technical, institutional, and behavioral strata in Generative AI systems.

3   Ethical Tensions in Generative AI

This chapter introduces a three-dimensional ethical tension model—Cognition–Behavior–Governance (CBG)—to explain the interactions and amplifications of these tensions throughout the lifecycle of Generative AI. The model views risks as systemically interconnected, emerging from the reinforcement of cognitive misunderstandings, behavioral shifts, and regulatory delays. It also provides the ethical basis for governance and responsibility mechanisms discussed in subsequent chapters.

3.1   Structural Fractures Across Cognition, Behavior, and Governance

At the cognitive level, many users misinterpret how Generative AI systems operate, attributing understanding or intent to models like ChatGPT or Midjourney. This leads them to accept outputs as authoritative, especially in education or research contexts. Crucially, users often overlook their own co-authoring role—prompts encode value-laden frames that shape outcomes. Without recognizing this, users disengage from ethical responsibility and assume a passive stance.

At the behavioral level, interactions frequently drift into adversarial or strategic manipulation. Users may deliberately prompt for extreme or controversial content—for entertainment, virality, or ideological expression—using tactics like jailbreaks or prompt engineering to bypass safeguards. Such behaviors exploit model vulnerabilities and introduce ethical and safety risks that remain largely unaddressed by current interface design and policy frameworks.

At the governance level, platforms and regulators lack mechanisms to audit or allocate accountability across the generative process. Governance remains focused on reactive output moderation, offering little in terms of upstream behavioral feedback or prompt-level intervention. Ethical responsibility is rarely contextualized or enforced, leaving cognitive biases, behavioral misuse, and institutional oversight disconnected.

Together, these dimensions form a reinforcing loop: user misunderstanding fosters risky behavior; normalized misuse weakens platform design standards; and regulatory gaps fail to restore ethical boundaries. Over time, this loop generates systemic ethical instability across Generative AI environments.

To address this, Sect. 3.2 introduces a structured interaction model that visualizes these dynamics and supports the design of integrated governance mechanisms.

3.2 The CBG Ethical Tension Model

To capture the structural nature of ethical risks in Generative AI, we present a three-dimensional model—Cognition–Behavior–Governance (CBG)—that explains how user misconceptions, prompting behavior, and governance gaps interact and reinforce one another.

This model conceptualizes these dimensions not as isolated variables but as mutually reinforcing forces. When users misunderstand how generative models function, they may engage in ethically risky prompting. Such behavior, if normalized and unregulated, entrenches misconceptions and undermines platform safeguards. Weak or delayed governance further amplifies these effects—creating a recursive loop of ethical instability.

As shown in Fig. 1, the CBG model visualizes this triangular dynamic: misaligned cognition encourages misuse; misuse erodes interface-level accountability; and governance inertia magnifies both. The result is a system-level diffusion of responsibility, opacity in ethical causality, and weakened normative control.

By focusing on upstream stages—especially the prompt–generation interface—this model highlights where governance can be most effective. It also provides the conceptual foundation for the embedded governance mechanisms proposed in Sect 4, and the reaffirmation of human agency explored in Sect 5.

Fig. 1. Three-Dimensional Ethical Tension Model for Generative AI.

4 A Multi-Layered Governance Framework

4.1 From Theory to Structure: Embedded Governance Principles

The ethical risks of Generative AI are not isolated incidents but systemic outcomes across the prompt–generation–accountability chain. Unlike traditional AI risks, which typically arise from discrete algorithmic failures, Generative AI generates distributed ethical challenges through recursive user–system interactions. Addressing these risks requires more than ex-post regulation or static policy—it demands a governance model embedded within the system's architecture.

We adopt the theory of embedded governance, as developed by Floridi and Cowls [34], which argues that ethical oversight should be pre-integrated into the technological infrastructure rather than added post-deployment. This means reimagining governance not as external policing, but as a normative property of platform design, interface logic, and user interaction. Ethics must become an internalized aspect of system behavior.

Based on this principle, we propose a four-layered governance framework spanning the state, platforms, organizations, and users. Each layer targets a specific zone of responsibility: governments define legal boundaries and auditing structures; platforms mediate prompt inputs and generative outputs; organizations establish standards; and users actively co-construct ethical outcomes. These layers are interdependent, forming a recursive structure where ethical risks and responsibilities circulate and reinforce one another.

While our framework draws on Value-Sensitive Design (VSD), it also addresses its limitations. VSD, as outlined by Friedman and Hendry [28] and van den Hoven et al. [27], emphasizes stakeholder inclusion during system design. Yet, it presumes stable actor roles and system boundaries—assumptions that falter in Generative AI contexts. Here, users simultaneously prompt, interpret, and shape outputs, while system responses remain emergent and dynamic. Critiques by Søraker et al. [29] and Liu et al. [30] highlight that VSD lacks runtime adaptability for ethical traceability, user contestability, and behavioral intervention.

Our framework advances these ideas by embedding ethical mechanisms into live system operations. Features like prompt logging, semantic dashboards, generation path mapping, and layered explainability embed ethics into everyday interaction. These tools shift ethics from principle to practice—visible, adaptive, and aligned with user agency.

As illustrated in Fig. 2, the four governance layers converge to form an integrated system for both top-down policy oversight and bottom-up ethical engagement. This structure enables scalable and actionable governance that reflects the complex ecology of Generative AI, and empowers all actors—users, developers, and institutions—to participate in maintaining ethical alignment.

4.2 Institutional and Platform-Level Mechanisms

Institutional and platform mechanisms constitute the operational backbone of embedded governance in Generative AI. While ethical values may be normatively articulated, they must be implemented through legal constraints, interface structures, and real-time user tools.

At the institutional level, national and international bodies have begun to formalize risk management strategies. The U.S. NIST AI Risk Management Framework [35] emphasizes transparency and lifecycle auditing, while Canada's CIFAR initiative promotes pre-deployment ethical assessments [36]. However, these frameworks fall short in addressing the emergent, co-constructed nature of Generative AI outputs. We propose four complementary measures: (1) define legal boundaries for prompt behavior, (2) enforce prompt-to-output traceability, (3) stratify accountability across actors, and (4) implement provenance labeling of AI-generated content.

Platforms, as intermediaries between user input and model output, are equally critical. Most current systems rely on back-end moderation with limited proactive guidance.

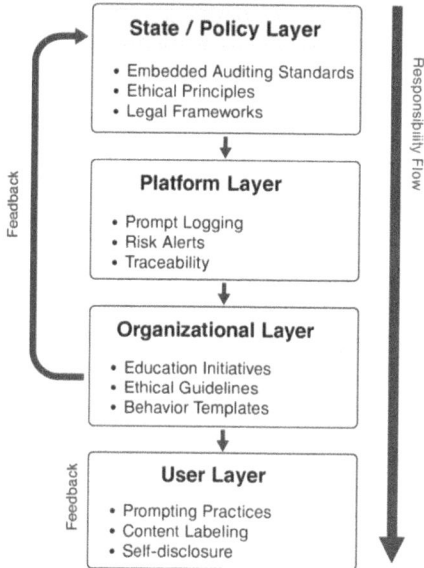

Fig. 2. Multi-Layered Governance Framework for Generative AI.

We advocate a shift to embedded, interface-level governance. Four mechanisms are recommended: (1) prompt behavior logging, (2) generation path mapping, (3) risk-sensitive feedback, and (4) user-facing ethical dashboards [37].

These proposals are supported by existing research. Henin et al. define "ethical UX friction" as deliberate design cues that slow user input to enhance reflection [38]. Rader et al. caution that overly smooth interfaces may foster automation bias [39], while Aroyo et al. advocate layered explainability tailored to user context [40]. These findings underscore the importance of interactive nudging mechanisms to shape behavior during prompt construction—not after content generation.

Preliminary empirical evidence supports this approach. GitHub Copilot uses inline warnings and session logging. Notion AI enables semantic tagging for output adjustments. ChatGPT and Bard include edit histories and source previews. Though limited, such features validate the feasibility of ethical interface design in practice.

Ultimately, institutions offer normative direction, while platforms translate those norms into operational practice. Their integration, as illustrated in Fig. 2, enables a scalable model of governance responsive to the dynamic ethics of Generative AI.

4.3 Organizational Roles and Ethical User Engagement

Organizations such as universities, publishers, and research institutions function as intermediaries of embedded AI governance. They mediate accountability by structuring workflows and codifying responsibility within professional practices.

We propose three mechanisms: (1) prompt disclosure templates, (2) ethics workshops to develop prompt norms, and (3) co-signature systems for shared authorship in AI-assisted work. Ibáñez and Olmeda [41] highlight the success of institutions that embed audits and transparency tools. Morley et al. [42] find that interdisciplinary review protocols and training foster role clarity and shared responsibility.

At the user level, governance should empower ethical agency rather than merely constrain misuse. We identify three key strategies: nudging, embedded education, and value-aligned feedback.

First, platforms should provide real-time prompting guidance. Chen et al. [43] show that visual cues and scaffolds help users generate more intentional prompts. Tools like history indicators and risk meters can help prevent misuse without limiting creativity.

Second, ethics education should be integrated into user interfaces. Hill and Narine [44] demonstrate that labeled examples and risk-aware checklists enhance user literacy. Zhang [45] finds that human-centered explainability promotes ethical awareness through interface design.

Third, feedback loops must reinforce responsible behavior. Lee and Han [46] show that adaptive nudging and accountability signals, such as tags and disclaimers, enhance ethical sensitivity over time. These tools support longitudinal engagement, embedding governance into everyday interaction.

Together, these interventions reposition users as ethical participants in co-creation, shifting the locus of responsibility from post-hoc enforcement to continuous, interface-mediated reflection.

5 Human Agency and the Right to Judgement

5.1 Philosophical Foundation of Expressive and Judgemental Rights

As Generative AI systems are increasingly integrated into high-trust domains such as education, journalism, science, and public administration, AI-generated content is often taken for granted as a legitimate form of expression—or even as reasoned assertion. However, behind this trend lies a fundamental ethical dilemma: in an AI-led chain of expression and reasoning, do humans still retain substantial expressive sovereignty and the final right to judgement? This is not merely a question of technical access, but a deeper philosophical concern about human ethical agency.

Kant views judgment not merely as rule application, but as a core exercise of rational autonomy and free will. Judgement is grounded in the human capacity to set ends and values autonomously. Any tendency to automate or outsource this process undermines that very autonomy and thus indirectly weakens human freedom [47].

Similarly, Charles Taylor argues in Sources of the Self that expression is a form of ethical practice through which individuals locate themselves in the world, define their value orientation, and articulate moral beliefs [48]. Expression is not mere information delivery—it is a process of self-positioning within social context. In Generative AI scenarios, when expression is reduced to prompt engineering, the inner ethical and value-laden dimensions of expression risk being erased.

Hannah Arendt, in Responsibility and Judgment, goes further by defining judgement as the capacity to offer ethical responses in public life under conditions of normative ambiguity [49]. While Generative AI can simulate context-sensitive logic and coherence, it lacks the moral architecture to engage in value-based deliberation or bear ethical consequences. In this sense, AI outputs may be logical, but they are never truly accountable.

Philosopher Mark Coeckelbergh emphasizes that once AI becomes embedded in moral action, human behavior is inevitably implicated in a shared responsibility network [50]. Yet shared responsibility does not imply substitution. Even as technology mediates or co-produces expression and judgement, mechanisms must exist to preserve the human capacity to set values and exercise evaluative control. Otherwise, the ethical chain of social responsibility collapses into ambiguity.

Therefore, we must assert human sovereignty over expression and judgement at three levels: technical, ethical, and institutional. Only by doing so can Generative AI systems maintain a legitimate "human-centered" ethical foundation, rather than eroding agency in the name of efficiency or fluency.

5.2   Institutional Mechanisms for Affirming Human Agency

To respond to the above philosophical tensions and embed expressive and judgemental sovereignty into Generative AI systems, this study proposes three practical mechanisms: the right to interrupt generation, the right to contest output, and the right to attribute human oversight. These mechanisms address critical touchpoints where human agency is at stake—from interaction to interpretation to dissemination. Furthermore, each mechanism aligns with the governance roles of platforms, organizations, and states.

First, the right to interrupt generation refers to the user's ability to intervene, redirect, or terminate AI output during the generative process. Technically, platforms should support real-time semantic previews, editable prompt visualization interfaces, and adjustable generation control channels. These affordances ensure user control over content direction and help prevent deviation from intended communicative goals.

Second, the right to contest output ensures that users can reject, dispute, or annotate AI-generated results. In domains with high standards of responsibility—such as research and education—institutions should implement mechanisms for human-in-the-loop review. These include visible annotations of human judgment, retrievable prompt logs, and generation traceability protocols. Such tools increase the visibility of human evaluative behavior and foster social trust.

Third, the right to attribute human oversight mandates that all publicly disseminated AI content should be labeled according to three criteria: whether it was reviewed by a human, whether the prompt strategy was user-defined, and whether the content was modified or rejected. National regulatory bodies should promote these practices via a standardized AI content transparency labeling system, allowing the public to trace responsibility chains in human–machine collaborations.

This triadic mechanism not only offers technical feasibility but also aligns with the "Cognition–Behavior–Governance" tension model in Sect. 3 and the multi-layered embedded governance framework introduced in Sect. 4. It bridges philosophical reflection with institutional design, reinforcing a human-centered approach to Generative AI development.

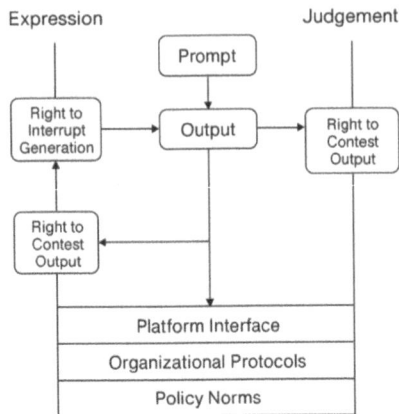

Fig. 3. Ethical and Institutional Mechanism for Confirming Human Agency in Generative AI Systems.

6 Conclusion

Generative AI is fundamentally reshaping how meaning is produced and decisions are made. Its risks—spanning misinformation, bias, and responsibility gaps—are not isolated flaws but systemic effects emerging from the interaction between user cognition, prompt behavior, and governance structures.

This study presents three integrated contributions. First, it introduces the Cognition–Behavior–Governance (CBG) model to conceptualize how ethical risks in Generative AI are reinforced through feedback loops across these dimensions. Second, it proposes a multi-layered governance framework, embedding ethical accountability at the levels of state, platform, organization, and user, shifting the focus from output moderation to structural design. Third, it affirms human agency in AI interaction by advocating for three rights—interruption, contestation, and oversight—as mechanisms to preserve expressive and judgmental sovereignty.

Together, these contributions form a coherent ethical response pathway, supported by Fig. 1 (CBG model), Fig. 2 (governance layers), and Fig. 3 (agency framework). The proposed model is both theoretically grounded and institutionally applicable.

Future work should develop context-specific governance metrics, real-time risk forecasting tools for multimodal outputs, and cross-cultural evaluations of ethical alignment to enhance inclusivity and adaptability.

At this turning point in technological development, ethics must be designed into AI systems—not applied after the fact. Centering human agency remains essential to ensuring AI innovation serves democratic, accountable, and humane futures.

Acknowledgments. This study was funded by 2024 Hunan Provincial Department of Education Scientific Research Project (grant number 24C0600).

Disclosure of Interests. The authors declare that they have no known competing financial interests or personal relationships that could have appeared to influence the work reported in this paper.

References

1. Li, C., Jurgens, J.: We must come together to ensure an AI future that works for all. World Economic Forum (2023). https://www.weforum.org/agenda/2023/07/we-must-come-together-to-ensure-an-ai-future-that-works-for-all/

2. Bick, A., Blandin, A., Deming, D.J.: The rapid adoption of generative AI. Federal Reserve Bank of St. Louis – On the Economy Blog (2024). https://www.stlouisfed.org/on-the-economy/2024/apr/rapid-adoption-generative-ai

3. Kwong, J.C.C., Leung, K., Chung, M.H., et al.: The long but necessary road to responsible use of large language models in healthcare research. NPJ Digit. Med. **7**, 177 (2024). https://doi.org/10.1038/s41746-024-01060-4

4. Dunne, T.: ChatGPT: these are not hallucinations – they're fabrications and falsifications. Schizophr. **9**, 133 (2023). https://doi.org/10.1186/s40479-023-00251-8

5. Hu, T., Liang, W., Liu, Y., Peng, Y., Kim, J., et al.: Generative language models exhibit social identity biases. Nat. Comput. Sci. **5**, 65–75 (2025). https://doi.org/10.1038/s43588-024-00500-6

6. UNESCO: Generative AI: UNESCO study reveals alarming evidence of regressive gender stereotypes. UNESCO Press Release (2024). https://www.unesco.org/en/articles/generative-ai-gender-bias

7. Chiba-Okabe, H., Su, W.J.: Tackling copyright issues in AI image generation through originality estimation and genericization. Sci. Rep. **15**, 10621 (2025). https://doi.org/10.1038/s41598-025-56081-2

8. Gilbert, S.: The EU passes the AI act and its implications for digital medicine are unclear. npj Digit. Med. **7**, 135 (2024). https://doi.org/10.1038/s41746-024-00999-3

9. UNESCO: recommendation on the ethics of artificial intelligence. UNESCO Global Standard-Setting Instrument (2021). https://unesdoc.unesco.org/ark:/48223/pf0000381137

10. Segal, A.: NIST's AI risk management framework plants a flag in the AI debate. Brookings Institution Report (2023). https://www.brookings.edu/articles/nists-ai-risk-management-framework-plants-a-flag-in-the-ai-debate/

11. Novelli, C., Andreasson, M., Degli Esposti, P.: Personalism in generative AI deployment: deciding ethically when human creative expression is at stake. Humanist. Manag. J. **9**, 1–15 (2024). https://doi.org/10.1007/s41463-024-00139-z

12. Rettberg, J.W.: How Generative AI endangers cultural narratives. Issues Sci. Technol. (2024). https://issues.org/generative-ai-cultural-narratives-rettberg/

13. Degli Esposti, P., Novelli, C., Andreasson, M.: Art without artists? Human expression and generative AI. Humanist. Manag. J. **9**, 16–28 (2024). https://doi.org/10.1007/s41463-024-00140-6

14. Nature Editorial Board: Stop talking about tomorrow's AI doomsday when AI poses risks today. Nature **618**, 492 (2023). https://doi.org/10.1038/d41586-023-01523-8

15. U.S. Government Accountability Office: Science & tech spotlight: Generative AI (GAO-23-106782). U.S. GAO Report (2023). https://www.gao.gov/assets/gao-23-106782.pdf

16. Marcus, G.: Artificial confidence: even the newest AI models produce misinformation. Science **379**(6637), 1138–1139 (2023). https://doi.org/10.1126/science.adh5265

17. Tamkin, A., et al.: Understanding the capabilities, limitations, and societal impact of large language models. ACM Comput. Surv. **55**(12), 1–41 (2023). https://doi.org/10.1145/3571730

18. Birhane, A., et al.: Multimodal datasets: misogyny, pornography, and malignant stereotypes. Patterns **2**(10), 100423 (2021). https://doi.org/10.1016/j.patter.2021.100423

19. Raji, I.D., et al.: Closing the AI accountability gap: defining an end-to-end framework for internal algorithmic auditing. In: Proceedings of ACM FAccT'22, pp. 33–44 (2022). https://doi.org/10.1145/3531146.3533112

20. Shin, D.: Debiasing AI: Institutional, Human, and Algorithmic Approaches. CRC Press, Taylor & Francis (2023). https://doi.org/10.1201/9781003530244

21. Samuelson, P.: Allocating ownership rights in computer-generated works. Commun. ACM **65**(7), 32–35 (2022). https://doi.org/10.1145/3528081

22. Menell, P.S., Lemley, M.A.: Intellectual property and the artificial intelligence revolution. Berkeley Technol. Law J. **36**(4), 1237–1300 (2021)

23. Chesterman, S., et al.: Artificial intelligence and the limits of legal personality. Int. Comparative Law Quart. **69**(4), 819–844 (2020). https://doi.org/10.1017/S00205893200 00366

24. Abbott, R., Bogenschneider, B.: Should robots pay taxes? Tax policy in the age of automation. Harvard Law Policy Rev. **12**(1), 145–175 (2020)

25. Binns, R., et al.: Human rights by design: the responsibilities of social media platforms to address harmful content. ACM Trans. Soc. Comput. **3**(2), 1–26 (2020). https://doi.org/10.1145/3406117

26. Rudolph, J., Tan, S., Tan, S.: ChatGPT: Bullshit Spewer or the end of traditional assessments in higher education? J. Appl. Learn. Teach. **6**(1), 1–22 (2023). https://doi.org/10.37074/jalt.2023.6.1.9

27. Floridi, L.: AI as a public service: learning from Amsterdam and Helsinki. Philos. Technol. **33**(4), 541–546 (2020). https://doi.org/10.1007/s13347-020-00434-3

28. Danaher, J.: Axiological futurism: the systematic study of the future of values. Futures **132**, 102780 (2021). https://doi.org/10.1016/j.futures.2021.102780

29. Van den Hoven, J., Vermaas, P.E., van de Poel, I.: Design for Values: An Introduction. Springer, Cham (2022). https://doi.org/10.1007/s10676-023-09700-2

30. Friedman, B., Hendry, D.G.: Value Sensitive Design: Shaping Technology with Moral Imagination. MIT Press, Cambridge (2019)

31. Umbrello, S., van de Poel, I.: Mapping value sensitive design onto AI for social good principles. AI and Ethics **1**(3), 283–296 (2021). https://doi.org/10.1007/s43681-021-00038-3

32. Liu, Y., Yao, S., Raji, I.D.: Operationalizing VSD in generative AI platforms: a responsibility-centered critique. In: Proceedings of ACM Conference on Fairness, Accountability, and Transparency (FAccT 2024). https://doi.org/10.1145/3613904.3642810

33. Eaton, S. E., Anselmo, L., Toye, M. A.: A review of the scholarly literature on GPT and ChatGPT: implications for research, teaching, and learning. J. Educ. Thought **56**(1), 27–50 (2023). https://doi.org/10.11575/PRISM/40518

34. Floridi, L., Cowls, J.: A unified framework of five principles for AI in society. Harvard Data Sci. Rev. **3**(1) (2021). https://doi.org/10.1162/99608f92.8cd550d1

35. National Institute of Standards and Technology (NIST). (2023). AI Risk Management Framework 1.0. https://doi.org/10.6028/NIST.AI.100-1

36. CIFAR. Building Trust in Artificial Intelligence: Foundations for Governance (2023). https://cifar.ca

37. Raji, I.D., et al.: Closing the AI accountability gap: defining an end-to-end framework for internal algorithmic auditing. In: ACM Conference on Fairness, Accountability, and Transparency (2022). https://doi.org/10.1145/3442188.3445935

38. Hagendorff, T.: The ethics of AI ethics: an evaluation of guidelines. Mind. Mach. **30**(1), 99–120 (2020). https://doi.org/10.1007/s11023-020-09517-8

39. Rader, E., Cotter, K., Brandimarte, L.: Interfaces and illusions: how AI design shapes trust and ethical awareness. Big Data Soc. **10**(1) (2023). https://doi.org/10.1177/20438869231178844

40. Aroyo, L., Welty, C., Treude, C., et al.: Explainability for AI decision making: a practitioner's perspective. In: Holzinger, A. et al. (eds.) Human-Centric Machine Learning. Lecture Notes in Computer Science, vol. 12663, pp. 197–217. Springer, Cham (2021). https://doi.org/10.1007/978-3-030-85616-8_36

41. Ibáñez, J.C., Olmeda, M.V.: Operationalising AI ethics: how are companies bridging the gap between practice and principles? BMC Med. Ethics **24**, 10 (2023). https://doi.org/10.1186/s12910-023-01000-0

42. Morley, J., Kinsey, L., Elhalal, A., Garcia, F., Ziosi, M., Floridi, L.: Operationalising AI ethics: barriers, enablers and next steps. Artif. Intell. Rev. **57**, 1177–1198 (2023). https://doi.org/10.1007/s10462-024-10740-3

43. Chen, C., Lee, S., Jang, E., Sundar, S.S.: Is your prompt detailed enough? Exploring the effects of prompt coaching on users' perceptions, engagement, and trust in text-to-image generative AI Tools. In: Proceedings of Second International Symposium on Trustworthy Autonomous Systems (TAS '24), ACM, Austin, USA, 12 p. (2024). https://doi.org/10.1145/3686038.3686060

44. Hill, P.A., Narine, L.K.: Ensuring responsible and transparent use of generative AI in extension. J. Extension **61**(2), 13 (2023). https://doi.org/10.34068/joe.61.02.13

45. Zhang, J.: User interface design based on human-centered explainable AI methods. Master's Thesis, Utrecht University (2022). https://aaltodoc.aalto.fi/items/d9787946-2547-4d9b-806b-84b9160981c1

46. Lee, M., Han, S.: Human-AI collaboration through value-aligned nudging: enhancing responsible use of generative AI via interface design. Artif. Intell. Rev. (2024). https://doi.org/10.1007/s10462-024-10740-3

47. Kant, I.: Critique of the power of judgment. In: Guyer, P., Matthews, E. (ed.) Cambridge University Press (2000)

48. Taylor, C.: Sources of the Self: The Making of the Modern Identity. Harvard University Press (1989)

49. Arendt, H.: Responsibility and Judgment. Schocken Books (2003)

50. Coeckelbergh, M.: AI Ethics. MIT Press (2020)

Haptic Zoo: A Symphony of Multi-sensory Design to Bridge the Gap in Parent-Child Interaction for Visually Impaired Parents

Shican Zhou[1] ⓘ, Shupei Huo[1], Mingyue Gu[1], Anchu Yu[1], Zhixuan Yang[2], Mingyue Guo[3], Run Ye[4(✉)] ⓘ, Yujie Zhou[4] ⓘ, Qi Xu[1], and Cheng Yao[4]

[1] Hangzhou Dianzi University, Hangzhou 310018, China
[2] Jiangsu Normal University, Xuzhou 221116, China
[3] Qingdao Agricultural University, Qingdao 266000, China
[4] Zhejiang University, Hangzhou 310027, China
runye@zju.edu.cn

Abstract. Visually impaired parents encounter significant barriers in parent-child interactions due to sensory asymmetry and insufficient assistive tools, leading to imbalanced roles and weakened emotional bonds. This paper presents Haptic Zoo, a modular multi-sensory toy system designed to bridge tactile-auditory collaboration between visually impaired parents and sighted children. Through semi-structured interviews with 20 families and user experiments involving 19 families, we identified key design goals: enhancing accessibility via tactile markers and audio feedback, integrating multi-sensory engagement, and fostering role-balanced collaboration. The prototype employs 3D-printed textured components, magnetic connections with audible clicks, and RFID-triggered audio rewards. Quantitative results from adapted usability scales (UPEQ) and behavioral coding (IOS) demonstrated high usability and emotional bonding. Qualitative findings revealed improved collaborative dynamics, mutual empowerment through sensory complementarity, and reduced frustration. Haptic Zoo transforms sensory asymmetry into a collaborative advantage, offering design guidelines for inclusive, role-based toys. This study contributes to inclusive HCI research by addressing the overlooked needs of visually impaired parents and offering design guidelines for role-based collaborative toys.

Keywords: Parent-Child Interaction · Visually Impaired Parents · Multi-sensory Design

1 Introduction

The United Nations' *Convention On The Rights Of Persons With Disabilities (CRPD)* asserts that individuals possess the right to parent in a manner that is equal to that of others, irrespective of any disability [1]. Visually impaired parents face structural barriers in parent-child interactions, including the lack of visual cues, social biases [2],

R. Yamanishi et al. (Eds.): ICEC 2025 Workshops, LNCS 15935, pp. 120–131, 2025.
https://doi.org/10.1007/978-3-032-02534-0_12

and insufficient assistive resources, which collectively diminish their parenting self-efficacy [3] and exacerbate asymmetric parent-child roles and emotional detachment risks [4]. Research indicates that age-appropriate play significantly promotes children's socio-emotional and cognitive development while strengthening parent-child attachment [5]. However, visually impaired parents struggle to engage due to their inability to visually observe their children's activities [6], relying instead on tactile contact and verbal communication to compensate for missing visual information [7], further complicating emotional bonding.

Despite the recognized importance of parent-child play [8], existing studies on multi-sensory interactions and educational toys primarily focus on individual child experiences or designs for visually impaired children, overlooking the asymmetric collaboration needs between visually impaired parents and sighted children [9, 10]. The field of Human-Computer Interaction (HCI) also pays limited attention to the roles of visually impaired parents in collaborative play [10, 11], while mainstream toy designs remain visually dominant, lacking multi-sensory guidance and emotional feedback mechanisms [11], which restricts active participation from visually impaired parents.

To address these challenges, we propose Haptic Zoo, a modular multi-sensory toy set which supports asymmetric collaboration through tactile and auditory feedback channels. Combining semi-structured interviews, behavioural observations, and prototype validation, the research aims to: 1) provide design guidelines for role-based collaborative toys tailored to visually impaired families; 2) empirically validate the role of multi-sensory mechanisms in enhancing emotional connectedness; 3) introduce the case of visually impaired families into HCI research, broadening the understanding of play experiences in special-needs households.

2   Related Work

2.1   Parenting Dilemmas for Visually Impaired Parents

In recent years, research on parents with disabilities, particularly those with visual impairments, has deepened, primarily focusing on their psychological needs and social support challenges during parenting [12]. Studies indicate that sensory impairments not only undermine the family functionality and parenting effectiveness of visually impaired parents but also exacerbate their stress due to environmental barriers and insufficient institutional support [12]. In parenting practice, communication difficulties, limited access to educational information, and inadequate support services lead visually impaired parents to describe child-rearing as a constant struggle. Despite highly valuing their family roles, the lack of tailored support often triggers negative emotions such as anxiety and loneliness [13]. A cross-sectional study [14] reveals that visually impaired parents tend to rely on religious consolation or informal social networks to relieve stress; however, these avoidance-based strategies correlate negatively with life satisfaction, highlighting the fragility of their psychological support system. Additionally, the need to repeatedly prove their parenting competence in response to external doubts further burdens their mental health [13]. At the family structure level, children often assume additional caregiving roles, forming a secondary care phenomenon that, while maintaining family operations, increases children's emotional strain and social isolation among family members [15].

2.2 Parenting Practices and Interaction Patterns of Visually Impaired Parents

The parenting practices and parent-child interaction patterns of visually impaired parents are a key focus of special education and family research. Qualitative research [16] shows that visually impaired mothers use auditory monitoring and tactile perception to compensate for environmental information when caring for sighted children aged 0 to 3 years, thereby establishing a sense of overall parenting competence. Z. Moghadam et al. proposed the Close Nurturers model [3], emphasizing the use of multi-sensory methods such as vocal calls and tactile imagination to address parenting anxiety. Pagliuca et al. found that visually impaired parents rely on touch, smell, and social support networks for daily care tasks such as breastfeeding, feeding, and medication administration, demonstrating a high degree of environmental adaptability [17].

Regarding parent-child interaction, a comparative study [18] shows that the lack of vision prompts visually impaired mothers to enhance verbal interaction and physical touch to make up for the limitations of eye contact and facial expression communication. In game scenarios, visually impaired parents often replace the traditional dominant role with presence participation and strengthen the parent-child bond through emotional companionship, proving that non-visual interaction can maintain high-quality teaching and emotional interaction [4]. Early observational studies [19] also confirmed that non-verbal interactions such as physical games and sound responses can effectively maintain the quality of parent-child emotions, challenging the traditional concept that visual impairment inevitably leads to interaction disorders.

2.3 Status of Multi-Sensory Toy Design for Special Groups

In recent years, the design of multi-sensory integrated toys has rapidly advanced in the fields of special education and assistive technology, mainly focusing on tactile-visual composite stimulation, sensory compensation materials, and modular assembly structures [22, 23]. Existing studies have shown that tangible geometric toys with non-standard shapes can effectively increase the overall speech volume and spatial description of both parents and children [22]. In addition, innovative materials and technologies, such as sustainable cork and inclusive tactile reliefs have provided new paradigms for toy design for special groups [24]. The application of modular interlocking building blocks in advanced concept learning has been verified [25]. LEGO Braille Bricks and optical Braille blocks enable visually impaired and sighted children to play and learn together through Braille and audio prompts [26, 27]. However, most existing research focuses on blind children, or the usage scenarios of a single group. There is still a lack of design for haptic-oriented toys that allow visually impaired parents and sighted children to play together in a collaborative manner.

3   Formative Study

A formative research study was conducted to enhance comprehension of the behavioral characteristics, emotional dynamics, and practical barriers when parents with visual impairments interact with their sighted children, involving interviews with 20 groups of families composed of visually impaired parents and sighted children. Each group consists of one parent with visual impairment (11 males and 9 females, aged 31−51, M = 38.8, SD = 6.117) and one sighted child (11 boys and 9 girls, aged 3−10, M = 7.75, SD = 1.71), from three cities in China.

The study focused on the patterns of game participation, role perception, and willingness to cooperate within the family. Particular attention was paid to the participation status and potential of visually impaired parents in parent-child games, providing a basis for the development of haptic-oriented parent-child interactive toys.

3.1   Method

The formative study utilized a qualitative research approach centered around semi-structured interviews, each lasting 25−30 min. The content focused on specific themes, including parent-child interaction time and patterns, experiences of sharing toys, emotional experiences in the process of cooperation, children's perception of parents' abilities, and parents' expectations of an ideal parent-child cooperation relationship. All interviews were recorded and transcribed with the participants' written consent, and each participant group received a gift worth $5.

3.2   Key Findings

Based on the interview data, we have summarized the following key findings.

Insufficient Toy Accessibility Hinders Parent-Child Collaboration. Most families (e.g., Family 1, 2, 6, 12) noted that existing toys (e.g., LEGO, puzzles) posed operational challenges for visually impaired parents due to small parts and lack of tactile or auditory cues. For instance, Family 6 mentioned that during block assembly, "the father struggled to align parts due to poor vision, requiring the child to assist in locating components" while Family 12's child stopped inviting the mother to play as she could not see LEGO pieces clearly. Family 18 suggested adding tactile textures or auditory feedback to enhance accessibility.

Child-Led Play Conflicts with Parental Role Expectations. Parents generally desired equal collaboration (e.g., Family 1, 3, 5, 9), yet children often dominated play due to impatience or efficiency concerns (e.g., Family 1, 8, 12). For example, Family 1's child disliked spending time teaching the father during assembly, while Family 5's child rushed to finish building, limiting the father's involvement. Family 9's mother hoped for equal partnership, but the child perceived her as "clumsy" and preferred solo play.

Tactile and Auditory Enhancements Could Improve Interaction. Several families (e.g., Family 6, 13, 18, 19) highlighted that tactile or auditory enhancements could make toys more inclusive. For instance, Family 6's child desired toys with voice navigation or tactile bumps, while Family 19's parent wanted audio tutorials to confirm assembly accuracy. Family 7's visually impaired parent acknowledged LEGO's strong tactile experience but suggested enlarging pieces or adding sound to optimize collaboration.

3.3 Design Goals

Based on the insights gathered from the formative study, the following design goals have been established to guide the development of a parent-child co-play toy.

Enhance Toy Accessibility to Lower Operational Barriers. Integrate tactile markers (e.g., bumps, textures) and auditory feedback (e.g., voice guidance, sound cues) into toys, while enlarging component sizes (Families 7, 12). Tactile differentiation and audio instructions can help visually impaired parents navigate tasks independently, enabling collaborative play.

Integrate Multi-Sensory Feedback to Enhance Engagement. Combine tactile, auditory, and simple visual feedback. Multi-sensory interactions can both support accessibility for parents and enhance engagement for children, fostering mutual enjoyment (Families 6, 7, 19).

Design Collaborative Mechanics to Balance Roles. Develop interdependent task structures, such as division of labor (e.g., tactile assembly by parents, visual verification by children) or cooperative puzzles requiring dual input. Enforce collaborative rules (e.g., turn-taking, joint decisions) to align with parental desires for "equal partnership" (Families 3, 5).

4 Haptic Zoo

The Haptic Zoo is a multi-sensory interactive toy system for visually impaired parents and sighted children, integrating tactile recognition, auditory feedback, and role-based collaboration to foster emotionally rewarding play.

The toy system comprises five distinct animals, including a lion with a mane, an elephant with a trunk, a giraffe with a long neck, a sheep with wool, and a hippo with a belly. It also includes a contour-style themed map. Each animal comprises 6−9 modular parts (head, body, limbs, etc.) 3D-printed with PLA. Children assemble the outline (uniform wood-colored parts), while parents handle textured feature components (tactile patterns), differentiated by raised lines, grooves, and edges for tactile navigation [27]. Polarity-matched magnets connect modules, ensuring stability and providing audible clicks. The thematic mat adopts a contour style and is organized according to the natural habitats of different animals (see Fig. 1).

The implementation of Haptic Zoo is shown in Fig. 1(c). RFID tags are embedded in each animal, and the RC522 RFID module is embedded at the bottom of the corresponding position of the theme mat [28]. The primary control unit incorporates the Arduino UNO and the DFPlayer Mini audio module, functioning in a collaborative manner. Upon the completion of the animal assembly, the RFID module scans its respective tag number, which in turn activates the Arduino, prompting the DFPlayer to emit the designated

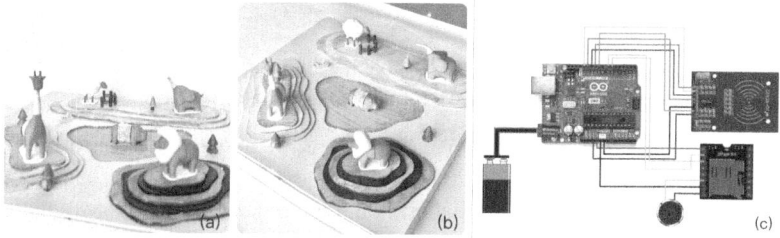

Fig. 1. (a, b) The design of Haptic Zoo, (c) Circuit diagram of each toy in Haptic Zoo

stage of positive voice feedback, such as "Dingdong, you have successfully awakened the Lion King!" (lion roar). This feature enables parents and children to receive immediate and perceptible feedback upon completion of each stage of the puzzle [29, 30]. Once all the animals have returned, the system will provide a summary and encouragement, reinforcing collaborative rituals [29].

5 User Experiment

5.1 Setup and Participants

This study recruited 19 families comprising visually impaired parents and their sighted children, meeting the inclusion criteria that at least one parent with total blindness or severe low vision and one child aged $3-10$ years (M $= 6.8$, SD $= 2.15$). The parent group included 7 males and 12 females, aged $30-51$ (M $= 39.1$, SD $= 6.35$), with 12 fully blind and 7 severely visually impaired individuals. The children (7 boys, 12 girls) were all in preschool or elementary school, demonstrating basic cognitive and collaborative abilities.

Experiments were conducted in a soundproof room equipped with a low-height table and fixed cameras. Each family used an identical Haptic Zoo system, with components disassembled and placed in an open container initially (see Fig. 2). Informed consent was verbally explained by researchers and confirmed via audio recording by participants. Sessions were video-recorded to capture behavioral, verbal, and emotional data, with all data anonymized. After the experiment, each family received $50 as a token of gratitude.

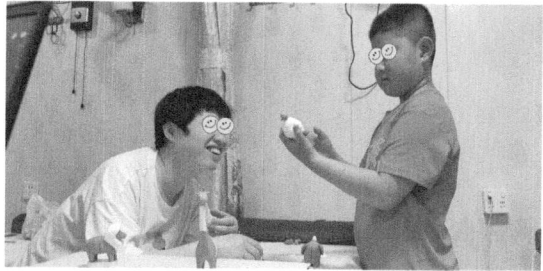

Fig. 2. Experiment participant's actual photo

5.2 Measures

This study employed a mixed-methods approach combining quantitative and qualitative measures to systematically evaluate the effectiveness of Haptic Zoo.

Quantitative Measures. For subjective experience, we adapted the Ubisoft Perceived Experience Questionnaire (UPEQ) [20] into parent and child versions. The parent scale included 5 dimensions (usability, collaboration, emotional bonding, educational value, overall satisfaction) with 3 items each, rated on a 5-point Likert scale (1 = strongly disagree, 5 = strongly agree). The child version retained the structure but simplified language. Researchers verbally administered items and recorded responses to accommodate visual impairments. For behavioral observation, the Interaction Observation Scale (IOS) [21] was used to code collaborative behaviors from video recordings. Two researchers independently scored behaviors on a 5-point frequency/intensity scale.

Qualitative Measures. For qualitative assessment, semi-structured interviews were conducted to gain in-depth understanding of user experiences, covering aspects such as task experience, role division, changes in parent-child relationship, design feedback, and future expectations. Open-ended questions were used for parents while child-friendly language and physical props were employed for children to ensure authentic and complete data collection. All interviews were audio-recorded, transcribed, and analyzed thematically through systematic coding.

5.3 Procedures

The experiment follows a 45-min protocol across three phases to balance natural interaction and structured data collection (see Fig. 3). First, brief pre-experiment interviews (10 min) with parents and children document daily play habits and pain points with traditional toys. Next, a 2-min orientation introduces Haptic Zoo's structure, assembly logic, and sound feedback, after which parent-child pairs collaborate freely with minimal researcher prompts (only for explicit help or prolonged delays). Finally, post-task measures include administering parent/child UPEQ scales (5 min) and semi-structured interviews (13 min) to capture usability feedback, collaborative experiences, and design preferences. Researchers ensure participant safety and comfort throughout, recording interactions for analysis.

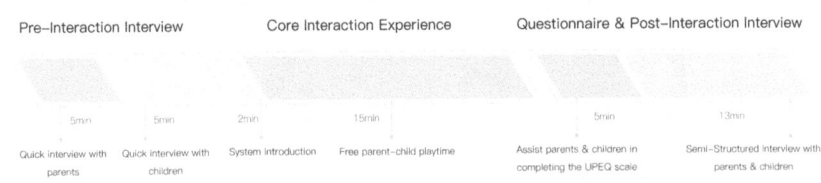

Fig. 3. The flow chart for one pair of participants

6 Results

6.1 Quantitative Analysis

The study recruited 19 families with visually impaired parents and sighted children. Quantitative analysis of the Ubisoft Perceived Experience Questionnaire (UPEQ) and Interaction Observation Scale (IOS) revealed significant outcomes across dimensions. For parent-rated UPEQ, the Ease of Use and Operability dimension (Items 1–3) showed high consistency (M = 4.51, SD = 0.76), with Item 3 (intuitive circuit feedback and sound trigger logic) scoring highest (4.79 ± 0.54). The Collaborative Experience and Interaction dimension (Items 4–6) exhibited moderate variability (M = 4.47, SD = 0.89), with Item 5 (frequent communication for task completion) scoring lowest (4.37 ± 0.96), indicating occasional coordination challenges. The Emotional and Relational Connection dimension (Items 7–9) achieved high scores (M = 4.59, SD = 0.63). The Educational and Cognitive Value dimension (Items 10–12) showed uniformly high ratings (M = 4.63, SD = 0.58), with Item 10 (child's active observation of shape-texture correspondence) at 4.79 ± 0.71. The Overall Satisfaction dimension (Items 13–15) demonstrated strong agreement (M = 4.91, SD = 0.34), especially Item 14 (toy improved interaction, 5.00 ± 0.00).

For child-rated UPEQ, the Ease of Use and Operability dimension (Items 1–3) had a mean of 4.56 ± 0.73, but Item 2 (clear operation steps) scored lower (4.05 ± 0.85). The Emotional and Relational Connection dimension (Items 7–9) showed exceptional consistency (M = 4.77, SD = 0.54), with Item 9 (child's trust and patience, 4.63 ± 0.60). The Educational and Cognitive Value dimension (Items 10–12) achieved high scores (M = 4.84, SD = 0.38), including Item 11 (understanding tactile information roles, 4.73 ± 0.56).

On IOS, the Interaction Frequency dimension (Items 1–2) had a mean of 4.46 ± 0.85, with Item 2 (physical contact frequency, 4.63 ± 0.57) higher than Item 1 (initiative communication, 4.29 ± 1.15). The Cooperative Collaboration dimension (Items 3–5) showed moderate performance (M = 4.22, SD = 0.97), with Item 4 (joint problem-solving, 3.89 ± 1.32) as the lowest. The Sensory Collaboration Effectiveness dimension (Items 6–8) had a mean of 4.47 ± 0.69, with Item 7 (parental tactile explanations, 4.18 ± 1.22) and Item 6 (child's visual descriptions, 4.28 ± 1.05) confirming effective sensory complementarity. The Emotional Expression dimension (Items 9–10) showed frequent positive emotions (M = 4.71, SD = 0.56) and rare negative emotions (reverse-scored M = 4.28, SD = 0.95). The Task Engagement dimension (Items 11–13) had high means (4.69 ± 0.54), with Item 11 (child's active part exploration, 4.79 ± 0.38) and Item 12 (parental guidance for independence, 4.24 ± 1.12) highlighting balanced autonomy and collaboration.

6.2 Qualitative Analysis

Based on semi-structured interviews and observational data from 19 families with visually impaired parents and sighted children, we found that most families (e.g., Groups 1, 3, 5, 6) spontaneously formed a collaborative division of labor between parents' tactile recognition and children's visual assembly, aligning with Haptic Zoo's dual-channel design. For instance, Group 6's father noted, "I distinguished parts by texture, and my child located them spatially", with parents focusing on tactile exploration (e.g., texture/shape differentiation) and children handling visual-spatial assembly, forming fluid collaboration through complementary sensory roles. Tasks with moderate challenges (e.g., loose sheep legs in Group 4) motivated joint problem-solving, with families reporting higher-than-expected enjoyment and emphasizing that "audio feedback upon success reinforced the sense of achievement" (Groups 2, 5, 8). Emotionally, children valued the sense of being needed and collaborative problem-solving (e.g., Group 9's child stated, "Helping Mom find parts made us feel awesome"), while parents felt understood through tactile cooperation (Group 7's mother mentioned, "My child patiently explained visual details, building trust").

However, perceptions of educational value diverged: Parents emphasized skill-building (e.g., Group 10's father highlighted "improved observation skills"), whereas children prioritized playfulness (e.g., Group 5's child favored "the lion module with instant sound feedback"). Notably, multi-sensory cues (e.g., magnetic clicks, voice prompts) reduced operational barriers, with Group 7's parent stating, "Auditory confirmation allowed independent validation", enhancing autonomy for visually impaired users. In summary, Haptic Zoo fostered equitable participation through role-based collaboration and sensory enhancements, though explicit educational alignment and adaptive difficulty require further refinement.

7   Discussion

7.1   Core Contributions and Sensory-Enhanced Collaboration

Haptic Zoo fills a critical gap in inclusive parent-child games by combining haptic-auditory feedback and role-based tasks, making three key contributions. Firstly, multi-sensory design effectively bridges sensory asymmetry: visually impaired parents use tactile textures to identify components, while children assemble them spatially through visual cues. This natural division of labor reduces reliance on visual dominance and supports independent and collaborative participation.

Secondly, the system redefines the collaborative dynamic by balancing the roles of parents and children. Unlike traditional toys where children usually take the lead due to their visual advantages, the interdependent tasks of Haptic Zoo promote equal cooperation. Parents feel that their tactile expertise is valued (UPEQ-parents item 9, $M = 4.84$), while children gain satisfaction from solving problems together, such as "helping to find parts makes us feel great", reflecting the enhancement of role equality and emotional involvement.

Third, by focusing on visually impaired parents - a long-neglected group, we expanded the field of Human-Computer Interaction. Audio feedback (such as animal sounds when successfully assembling) created a shared sign of achievement, significantly enhancing emotional connection (UPEQ-parents item 7, $M = 4.58$). These findings challenge the assumption that sensory impairments will hinder games, proving that intentional design can turn asymmetry into a collaborative advantage.

7.2 Insights into Asymmetric Interaction Dynamics

Haptic Zoo highlights sensory complementarity as a key enabler for equitable play. Sighted children's visual descriptions (IOS item 6, $M = 4.29$) and parents' tactile explanations (IOS item 7, $M = 4.18$) formed a reciprocal information loop, where each party's sensory strength compensated for the other's limitation. This mutually supportive model not only improves task efficiency, but also promotes deep understanding and trust (UPEQ-parents item 9, $M = 4.84$, UPEQ-children item 9, $M = 4.63$).

However, variability in collaboration (e.g., some families preferred simpler textures while others sought complex puzzles) indicates the need for adaptive design. Future iterations could include adjustable difficulty levels and modular components to accommodate diverse ages and abilities, ensuring sustained engagement across developmental stages.

8 Future Work and Conclusion

The Haptic Zoo system, designed as a multi-sensory collaborative toy, demonstrates the potential to bridge tactile-visual interaction between visually impaired parents and sighted children through modular assembly, role-based task division, and auditory feedback. Quantitative and qualitative findings from 19 family experiments confirm its efficacy in fostering equitable collaboration, enhancing mutual trust, and reshaping children's perceptions of their parents' non-visual capabilities.

Limitations persist. The restricted sample size and controlled experimental settings may constrain generalizability, while younger children's linguistic development could introduce bias in self-reported measures. Additionally, observer-dependent behavioral coding and the lack of longitudinal data warrant caution in interpreting sustained impacts. Future research should expand diversity (e.g., cross-cultural families, siblings, or multi-disability groups) and employ longitudinal studies to assess long-term effects on attachment and relational dynamics. Technically, integrating generative AI-assisted modules could enable adaptive difficulty scaling and personalized voice guidance, while embedding emotion recognition algorithms may further refine multi-modal feedback. Practically, deploying Haptic Zoo in inclusive classrooms, rehabilitation centers, and community hubs would test its scalability and societal value.

Beyond a product innovation, Haptic Zoo challenges conventional notions of disability-centric design by framing collaboration as a mutual empowerment process. Moving forward, we envision Haptic Zoo as a catalyst for redefining inclusive play, where multi-sensory experiences transcend accessibility to nurture dignity, understanding, and joy in diverse family ecosystems.

References

1. UN Homepage. https://social.desa.un.org/issues/disability/crpd/convention-on-the-rights-of-persons-with-disabilities-crpd#Fulltext
2. Gładyszewska-Cylulko, J.: Self-stigma in the visually impaired, Interdisciplinary Contexts of Special Pedagogy, No. 22, pp. 179–193. Adam Mickiewicz University Press, Poznań (2018)

3. Moghadam, Z., et al.: Parenting experiences of mothers who are blind in Iran: a hermeneutic phenomenological study. J. Vis. Impairment Blindness **111**(2), 113–122 (2017)

4. Szpiro, S., et al.: The benefits of asymmetric abilities: blind parents play related interactions with sighted children. Disabil. Soc. 1–25 (2024)

5. Yogman, M., et al.: A pediatric role in enhancing development in young children. Pediatrics **142**(3) (2018)

6. RNIB Homepage. https://www.rnib.org.uk/living-with-sight-loss/independent-living/parenting/resources-for-blind-or-partially-sighted-parents/

7. Chiesa, S., et al.: Communicative interactions between visually impaired mothers and their sighted children: analysis of gaze, facial expressions, voice and physical contacts. Child Care Health Dev. **41**(6), 1040–1046 (2015)

8. Ginsburg, K.R.: The importance of play in promoting healthy child development and maintaining strong parent-child bonds. Am. Acad. Pediatrics Committee Psychosoc. Aspects Child Family Health Pediatrics **119**(1), 182–191 (2007)

9. Kim, S.J.: Are Digital Children's Books Accessible to Blind Parents with Sighted Children? UC Irvine (2023)

10. Dickenson, K.: How Parents with Blindness or Low Vision Leverage Technology to Care for Their Children, UC Irvine (2023)

11. IDSA Homepage

12. Anderzén-Carlsson, A., et al.: Lived experiences of parents with deafblindness - not "a walk in the park". Disabil. Rehabil.1–12 (2024)

13. Dunne, A., Ryan, C.: Being a parent with a physical disability: a systematic review. Rehabilitation psychology (2024). https://doi.org/10.1037/rep0000590

14. Indiana, M.L., Sagone, E., Fichera, S.L.O.: are coping strategies with well-being in deaf and blind parents related? Eur. J. Investig. Health Psychol. Educ. **11**(4), 1422–1439 (2021)

15. Huus, K., et al.: Living an ordinary life - yet not: the everyday life of children and adolescents living with a parent with deafblindness. Int. J. Qual. Stud. Health Well-being **17**(1) (2022)

16. Shackelford, S.: Blind mothers' perceptions of their interactions and parenting experiences with their sighted infants and toddlers (2004)

17. Pagliuca, L.M.F., Uchoa, R.S., Machado, M.M.T.: Blind parents: their experience in care for their children. Revista Latino-Americana de Enfermagem **17**(2) 271–274 (2009)

18. Chiesa, S., Galati, D., Schmidt, S.: Communicative interactions between visually impaired mothers and their sighted children: analysis of gaze, facial expressions, voice and physical contacts. Child Care Health and Development, Child Care Health and Development (2015)

19. Collis, G.M., Bryant, C.A.: Interactions between blind parents and their young children. Child: Care Health Dev. **7**(1), 41–50 (1981)

20. Albert, B., Tullis, T.: Measuring the User Experience: Collecting, Analyzing, and Presenting Usability Metrics. 2nd edn. Morgan Kaufmann, San Francisco (2013)

21. Aron, A., et al.: Inclusion of other in the self scale and the structure of interpersonal closeness. J. Pers. Soc. Psychol. **63**(4), 596–612 (1992)

22. Verdine, B.N., et al.: Effects of geometric toy design on parent-child interactions and spatial language. Early Childhood Res. Q. **46**, 126–141 (2019)

23. Ma, M.-Y., Lee, Y.-H.: Children with autism and composite tactile-visual toys during parent-child interaction. Interact. Stud. **15**(2), 260–291 (2014)

24. Ferreira et al.: A sustainable cork toy that promotes the development of blind and visually impaired young children. Sustainability **16**(15), 6312 (2024)

25. Melaku, S., et al.: Interlocking toy building blocks as hands-on learning modules for blind and visually impaired chemistry students. J. Chem. Educ. (2016)

26. Baqai, A., Jan, M., Maher, R.R.: Optical braille blocks for visually impaired elementary education. Mehran Univ. Res. J. Eng. Technol. **40**(1), 205–214 (2021)

27. Barros, G., Correia, W., Teixeira, J.M.: Towards the effectiveness of 3D printing on tactile content creation for visually impaired users. Polymers **15**(9), 2180 (2023)
28. Karime, A., et al.: RFID-based interactive multimedia system for the children. Multimed. Tools Appl. (2011)
29. Ryan et al.: Self-determination theory and the facilitation of intrinsic motivation, social development, and well-being. Am. Psychol. **55**(1), 68–78 (2000)
30. Sweetser, P., Wyeth, P.: GameFlow: a model for evaluating player enjoyment in games. Comput. Entertain. **3** (2005)

Author Index

© IFIP International Federation for Information Processing 2025
Published by Springer Nature Switzerland AG 2025
R. Yamanishi et al. (Eds.): ICEC 2025 Workshops, LNCS 15935, p. 133, 2025.
https://doi.org/10.1007/978-3-032-02534-0

The manufacturer's authorised representative in the EU is Springer
Nature Customer Service Centre GmbH, Europaplatz 3, 69115 Heidelberg,
Germany. If you have any concerns regarding our products, please
contact ProductSafety@springernature.com

Printed and bound by CPI Group (UK) Ltd, Croydon, CR0 4YY

28/04/2026

02098542-0008